POCKET GUIDE TO
WICCA

PAUL TUITÉAN AND ESTELLE DANIELS

THE CROSSING PRESS
FREEDOM, CALIFORNIA

For information on bulk purchases or group discounts for this and
other Crossing Press titles, please contact our Special Sales
Manager at 800-777-1048 x214.

Visit our Web site on the Internet: www.crossingpress.com

Library of Congress Cataloging-in-Publication Data

Tuitéan, Paul.
    Pocket guide to Wicca / Paul Tuitéan and Estelle Daniels.
        p. cm.
    Includes bibliographical references.
    ISBN 0-89594-904-0
    1. Witchcraft--United States. I. Daniels, Estelle. II. Title.
BF1573.T85   1998
133.4'3--dc21   98-5017
                                           CIP

Contents

Preface

Depending on who's talking, Wicca is the fastest growing religion in the United States, a manifestation of an aging hippie lunatic fringe, a dangerous cult which seeks to undermine Christianity, the leading New Age movement, or a religious front for hard-core ecologists.

Though some truth may be found in the above statements, they don't have much to do with what Wicca really is or why Wiccans practice Wicca. Wicca, as a religion and as a lifestyle, is generally misunderstood. This book aims to clarify the practices and underlying beliefs of Wicca.

In modern times Wicca has been practiced for only a couple of generations. Today's Wiccans are for the most part ordinary people who draw their beliefs from ancient roots and apply them to the needs of modern life.

Shifting and changing, contemporary Wicca evolves as new adherents come in and make it their own. Wicca in the '90s is different from Wicca in the '50s. And because modern Wicca is receptive and inclusive, a succinct, clear definition is difficult. There are core beliefs and practices, which we will explore in some detail in these pages, but Wicca is ultimately, as you will see, what each individual makes it.

The New Age movement, preceded by the occult explosion in the 1960s, has made many of the ideas and practices of Wicca more or less mainstream. Today you can go to almost any bookstore and buy a deck of Tarot cards. Astrologers and psychic readers are as common as plumbers. Workshops at Christian-based conferences explore the Goddess, the feminine aspect of Deity. Retreats where you can learn about shamanism and discover your power animal are widely advertised and attract many seekers. Though not strictly Wiccan, all of these contain elements of Wicca.

After reading this book you will probably have some confusion about what is and what is not Wicca. Don't worry—many Wiccans have the same confusion! Estelle's Wicca is different from Paul's Wicca. If the co-authors cannot always agree, at least you can draw on both their perspectives, select practices appealing to you, sense the underlying spirit, and form your own sense, and perhaps your own experience, of Wicca.

Introduction

Wicca is a modern version of the original pre-Christian, European shamanic religious tradition. It is a Pagan religion, that is, a religion not Judeo-Christian in origin. The word Pagan comes from the Latin root, *paganus*, meaning "not of the city," or rural. Because Christianity spread most slowly in the outlying rural areas, it was the Pagans who were converted last—and sometimes incompletely—so their faith became a mixture of the old and new religions. Many local saints are Christianized versions of Pagan deities (like Saint Brigit), adapted so that locals would more easily integrate Christianity into their beliefs.

Wicca is earth-, nature-, and fertility-oriented; its followers worship at the turn of the seasons and at new and full moons. They generally acknowledge both male and female Deities, and believe in reincarnation, magick, and divination. While Wicca is a spiritual and philosophical path, it is first and foremost a Religion, termed "the Craft," meaning the craft of the wise.

The word Wicca has two possible sources. The first is the Anglo-Saxon "wic" or "wit," meaning wise or learned. A person "of the Wicca" was a person who had knowledge (usually of healing and herbs) which placed them apart from ordinary people. Another possible origin is the Celtic word "wick," which means to bend or be supple. Wiccans were people who bent as life and conditions warranted. In the story of the Oak and the Willow, the oak does not bend and is blown down in the storm, while the willow is supple, bends, and survives the storm with little damage. Another interpretation of wick, or bending, is "bending with your Will" as one does in the process of Magick.

While reading this book you will notice that certain words are capitalized because they have specific Wiccan connotations, for example, Witch, First Degree (of Initiation), and Out (being open about one's Wiccan affiliations).

Wicca is unique as a religion in that it lacks a doctrine imposed by a hierarchical organization, does not provide a bible or holy book to which Wiccans can turn for spiritual guidance and instruction, includes a number of Traditions, allows individuals to worship and practice by themselves, and significantly assumes that each person will develop and continue to refine their own belief system and spiritual practices.

An individual's practice tends to draw from the practices of other Wiccans with whom they interact. If a person lives in an area where there are several Wiccan-type groups, they have the luxury of choice. More often, there is only one existing small group and that becomes their model. Some estimate that up to half of practicing Wiccans practice solo, or solitaire. Most Wiccans are ecologically-minded in some way, are spiritual, seek knowledge and self-improvement, try to be tolerant and accepting of others, and are just "regular people."

The emphasis on individualism within Wicca is both a strength and a weakness. Wiccans are strongly encouraged to think for themselves, but they also sometimes suffer from numerous disagreements, which all that individualistic thinking can generate. Wiccans have a tendency to go off by themselves if they are not happy with the current state of things in the local coven, group, community or whatever. Therefore Wicca is not a strongly cohesive religion. One can be in a coven or other small group, and be very tightly-knit, but there may not be a lot of inter-group loyalty or cohesiveness. Still most Wiccans have more in common than they do differences, so they gather at Festivals or in larger groups for interaction, communication, and to share the benefits that larger communities offer. These gatherings tend to be more time-specific than permanent and ongoing.

Here is a list of a number of beliefs which most Wiccans hold in common. With all the differences, it is good sometimes to remind ourselves just how much we do have in common.

1. Dual polarity of Deity
2. Belief in reincarnation
3. Respect for all; human, animal, plant, mineral, celestial and spiritual kingdoms alike
4. Immanence of Deity
5. Respect for the Earth Mother
6. Turning the Wheel and changing seasons mark the Sabbats
7. Eight solar Sabbats and 12 or 13 lunar Esbats
8. Wicca is a free choice religion—no proselytizing
9. All Initiates are Priests and Priestesses
10. Equality of all sexes and races
11. Magickal Circle is used for worship and celebration
12. Education and learning are valued and continually pursued
13. Wicca is counter-culture and somewhat underground

This book provides a brief overview of Wicca including some history, common beliefs and practices, and a few simple techniques to begin training (as much as can be imparted in a book). It is certainly not complete, nor is it a primer for becoming a Wiccan. It will, however, give interested people a good idea of what being a practicing Wiccan is all about. Blessed Be.

A Brief History of Wicca

There are many myths and practices within Wicca related to the origins and lineage of various Wiccan Traditions and belief systems. Most of this knowledge we owe to Margaret Murray, Robert Graves, and other historians, scholars, and anthropologists. But the history of modern Wicca cannot be reliably documented before 1951 and the work of Gerald Gardner. The modern incarnation of Wicca is an amalgam of ceremonial magick, mysticism, theosophy and the spiritualist movement, Masonic practices, eastern religions and thought, fairy tales, mythologies, folklore and legends, divination, and individual imagination and belief.

There are Traditions which claim to derive or descend from original hereditary sources (for example the English Gardnerian and Alexsandrian, and the Italian Strega Traditions or Lineages). There are Traditions which were created by authors and published in books (Seax-Wicca, and Starhawkian, from Starhawk's book *The Spiral Dance*). And there are Traditions that have evolved their own distinctive characteristics over time (Eclectic Wicca). Some Traditions are schismatic, having broken away from other older, established traditions (Georgian, Blue Star, and Elite). Some Traditions are exclusive, providing teaching and training only to their initiates (Gardnerian and Alexsandrian), and some Traditions will teach almost anyone (Eclectic). Some Traditions require only self-recognition and proclamation to become an adherent (Dianic). Some Traditions recognize degrees of initiation and rank from other Traditions, some recognize degrees from non-Wiccan Traditions, and others only recognize their own.

GARDNERIAN WICCA

Gerald Gardner was a British Civil Servant who spent most of his career in India. When Gardner retired to England, he was initiated into Wicca through a group which called itself the New Forest Coven, headed by a woman called "Old Dorothy" Clutterbuck. This woman was a hereditary witch, and this Coven had been in existence for decades. Being a Civil Servant in India, Gardner was a Mason. He also had studied Oriental mysticism and related topics most of his life, and had written several books on those subjects.

Gardner blended the hereditary Witchcraft of the New Forest Coven, called Wicca, with Masonic-like ceremonies and a handful of other practices popularized in the Golden Dawn shortly before W.W.I, creating the religion we know today as Gardnerian Wicca. Gardner's religion did not spring full-blown, but evolved over a number of years, benefiting from several other contributors, Dion Fortune and Doreen Valiente being the two most notable.

Sorting Gardner's contributions from those of Dion Fortune and Doreen Valiente is difficult. However in 1949 Gardner published a book of fiction, *High Magic's Aid*, which detailed the workings of an English Coven at Lammas in 1940 who were trying to repel Hitler's forces magically. In Britain in 1951, the last witchcraft laws that mandated all witches be put to death for practicing witchcraft were repealed. Because of these laws, the witches in Britain have long been extremely secretive about their practices. In 1954 Gardner published a book, *Witchcraft Today*, about the practices of witches, which asserted that witchcraft was alive and well in Britain, and that Gardner himself was a witch.

Gardner became an instant celebrity and for the rest of his life flirted with the press and became the "official

Witch" of Britain. He eventually purchased a witchcraft museum on the Isle of Man, which he ran for some years. At the time of his death, Gardnerian Wicca (the label Gardnerian was first used by a personal enemy of Gerald's) was well established, with a schismatic offshoot (Alexsandrian Wicca) and a number of covens in Britain, Europe, and America.

Gardnerian Wicca is not the only type of Wicca said to have survived since the Burning Times, the days of the Inquisition and Witch Trials in Europe and America. But Gardnerian Wicca was the first to be widely publicized and published. Gardner's books and numerous interviews and articles about him served to bring the idea and the reality of practicing witches to the attention of the modern world. The publicity attracted many who wanted to join the movement and become traditional witches also. Though other traditions co-existed, it was Gardner who brought Wicca into the public view and thus he is known as the founder of modern Wicca.

Whether Gardner ever met and talked with Aleister Crowley (one of the most prominent and infamous occultists of the first half of this century, the self-styled "wickedest man in the world") about Crowley's practices and research into magick and the like is unproven, but probable. Crowley's books were widely available, and as he wrote a great deal about the practices of magick, Gardner almost certainly borrowed from Crowley, perhaps with Crowley's knowledge and blessings.

Stories abound about Gardner's quirks of character which became incorporated into his version of Wicca. Be that as it may, Gardnerian practices have validity and can be highly effective, with respect to the altering of consciousness and the raising of power.

Since 1951 many Wiccans have evolved and moved away from strict Gardnerianism. Eclectic Wicca is considered by some to be the most common form of Wicca in the U.S. today, though secrecy and confidentiality makes any attempt to count Wiccans in any given Tradition pure guesswork, at best. But all Wiccans owe a debt of gratitude to Gerald Gardner for making the practice of our religion possible in the modern world.

SIGNIFICANT BOOKS

On October 31, 1979, two books were published which contributed to the explosion of Wicca in the United States. One was *The Spiral Dance* by Starhawk, which detailed a religion of Goddess worship and personal and magickal celebration. This was a mass market book, which made information which had heretofore only been available to initiates or scholars, widely available. The second was *Drawing Down the Moon* by Margot Adler, which was a profile of Wiccans across the United States. It told of people actually practicing Wicca, what they did, and how they did it. These two books brought Wicca and Goddess worship to the attention of the masses. Those already practicing Wicca discovered they were far from alone. Those seeking out Wiccans discovered there were many people and types of Wicca out there.

Though popular, these were also serious books on the Craft. Before this, Sybil Leek had published a number of books, but only one, *The Complete Art of Witchcraft* (1971 Signet, New York), which dealt directly with the religion and practices of witchcraft, and it was not widely marketed. Other books, like *The Naked Witch*, sensationalized

Witchcraft and scarcely mentioned Wicca. Many of these earlier books were just rehashes in the "*Happy Hooker*" genre.

The Spiral Dance and *Drawing Down the Moon* were the first modern American books which treated the subject seriously as a religion and valid spiritual path. The occult revolution had begun ten years before, now the Wiccan revolution followed. Since 1979, literally countless books have been published on Wicca, witchcraft, spellworkings, Sabbats, and every other topic relevant to Wicca. The divination and occult books started to come in the late 1960s. The Craft books came in the early 1980s. Wicca provided a spirituality and religious framework to add to mere occultism.

MODERN GROUPS

Modern American Wicca derives mainly from two disparate lines: Gardnerians, and the Z Budapest "I am a Witch" (Dianic) school.

The Gardnerians, and through them the Alexsandrians and Elites (pronounced *Ee-lites*) are hierarchical, have initiations, degrees, and an established set of rituals and practices. These Traditions could be called the high ceremonial magick (or high church) versions of Wicca. A person must go through training and demonstrate ability before getting an initiation. Most of these groups are considered closed, that is they commonly require some sort of sponsorship, and that you make some sort of commitment before you can receive any training or membership. They are extremely secretive and will only share information with other properly credentialed initiates. They are also secretive about membership (more so than other Wiccan Traditions) and when and where they meet, and they can be very difficult to find, even if you know what you are looking for.

The Dianic groups are feminist in origin evolving mainly from the women's movement of the '70s, open generally to women only. They have loosely evolved from the teachings of women such as Z. Budapest, Starhawk, and many other feminists who are not quite so publicly prominent. They are Goddess-oriented, have few initiations or rules, and are more free-form in their beliefs and practices. With many of these groups, one need only to proclaim, "I am a Witch" three times (if only in front of one's own mirror) to be considered a member. They are often very much oriented toward public ritual, dance and song, and can have large rituals with people from many smaller groups. These groups occasionally advertise widely, especially at feminist bookstores and other places where women hang out. They range from simple "women's spirituality" groups, sometimes nominally "Christian," all the way to stridently feminist or lesbian separatist groups. Exploring women's spirituality is the main focus of these groups, and little, if any, magick is consciously practiced.

There are other Wiccan Traditions and lines which evolved over the years in response to the interests of others who wanted a religion which met their needs. Radical Faery Wicca is a gay men's tradition. There are Wiccans who worship the Greek pantheon, and Wiccans who follow Celtic traditions and pantheons (separate from the Druids, which is a distinct neo-Pagan religion by itself).

Then there are various Family Traditions or Fam-Trads, which are a set of beliefs and practices preserved by members of a family over the generations. What Old Dorothy Clutterbuck taught Gardner years ago in the Old Forest Coven, was her Fam-Trad.

Strega (which is Italian for witch) is an Italian Tradition descended from Ancient Roman beliefs. Diana is worshipped as the Goddess, and there is a mixture of herbal, healing, and folklore which accompanies these beliefs. The book, *Aradia, or the Gospel of the Witches*, by Charles G. Leland, transcribed from an amalgam of sources around 1900 is a main sourcebook for the Strega Tradition, though there are adherents who have had practices and lore passed down from their mothers and grandmothers.

There are also other Fam-Trads extant in the United States. Most true Fam-Trads are extremely secretive and totally closed to all but family members, and not all family members may receive training and knowledge. Some Fam-Trads only train one or two people in each generation. Some teach all their children, and offer more advanced training to those who express strong interest in continuing the training. Within mainstream Wicca there are individuals who may have been raised in a Fam-Trad and then also received training in another Wiccan Tradition, and now practice both.

FESTIVALS

In the late 1970s a phenomenon arose in the U.S. and Canada which contributed greatly to the explosion of Wicca. It was pagan festivals or gatherings. These festivals are large, usually outdoor, camping type events where people of Pagan and/or Wiccan beliefs get together and exchange information, beliefs, practices, and recipes. This personal interaction has been vital to the growth of Wicca as a religion (see page 48 for more information about festivals).

Religious Beliefs

Wicca as a religion is different from mainstream Judeo-Christian religion in that there are very few absolutes, little dogma or doctrine, but rather a more general guideline of beliefs which most Wiccans share in common. The Wiccan Rede, The Law of Three, and The Golden Rule are the three main principles which guide a Wiccan's life. They may seem simplistic, but the simpler the tenet, the more it applies to in everyday life.

THE WICCAN REDE

"An ye harm none, do what ye will." The Wiccan Rede (pronounced *reed*) is generally considered the main guiding tenet of Wicca. It mandates that you can do whatever you want, but only if it harms no one including yourself. This implies a person should always be aware of the myriad consequences of each action, and how others might feel or respond. It definitely does not give a person free rein to act without regard to consequences. Most Wiccans consider an action before actually doing anything. If harm might result from the action, they assess the various levels of harm and then choose the action which will likely cause the least harm, or offer the most benefit while harming the least. The Rede also helps a person not to take anything for granted. Following the Rede readily leads one to live ecologically and to tread lightly upon the Earth. One may become a vegetarian, adopt a mindset of waste not want not, and develop a disdain for the rat race and "keeping up with the Joneses." What constitutes "harm" is a popular topic for group discussion. Generally people agree that harm means negative actions; actions that affect others or oneself adversely.

Sometimes *not* acting can cause the greatest harm.

THE LAW OF THREE

"Whatever you do will return to you threefold." The Law of Three is used as a way of monitoring day-to-day behavior. It means that if you send love, you will receive love threefold, and if you send animosity or negativity, that too will return threefold. It is the main tenet which prevents Wiccans from "cursing" others. Because Wiccans do practice magick, there exists the possibility of putting that practice to unpleasant, restrictive, or retributive use. Wiccans are well schooled in what constitutes "black magick." When following the Law of Three, they will avoid it. Besides, most magick is used for personal self-development and is never as easy or instantaneous as that which Samantha—from the '60s TV show *Bewitched*—could call up with a twitch of her nose. Wiccans might occasionally wish for such powers, but none have gained them.

THE GOLDEN RULE

"Do unto others as you would have them do unto you." The Golden Rule is a corollary to The Law of Three and simply a good guideline to live by. Though people may want to be treated in widely differing ways, the Golden Rule mandates a person think about and take personal responsibility for their actions and the consequences of these actions. Wiccans don't have confession or absolution of sins; they are expected to face up to their actions and own up to their mistakes. If they do err, they examine what they did and why they did it, hopefully becoming more aware and avoiding such problems in the future. If possible, they set things right in the present.

THE NOTION OF DARKNESS

Most Wiccans acknowledge some sort of "Dark Side" to the universe. This may or may not include evil. Generally, what is considered to be "Light" or "Bright" is what is beneficial; it builds and creates. What is termed "Dark" is what is harmful, destroys, and tears down. One could also call these principles Creation and Entropy. Instead of equating all that is Dark with bad and evil, Wiccans understand that the Dark is an integral part of life and the Universe. For example, where would a garden be without compost? Yet compost is rot and decay, the process of breaking down to simpler chemical components. By the above definition, decay is Dark. But it also brings benefit. Death is a Dark process, yet it is an integral part of life. Our present society is death-denying. Wiccans worship death as a natural part of the Cycle of the Year. Therefore, Wiccans prefer to think of the Dark as a natural part of life, not to be feared or battled, but understood and respected for its essential role.

Evil, as it refers to human actions, is something different. Death and destruction are natural processes, but when they become specific actions to serve a personal end, they may be called evil. So perhaps evil is a phenomenon of intent. When a river floods and destroys a building, that is certainly "of the Dark," but it is a natural force, not from evil intent. But if someone dynamites a building, deliberately blowing it up to hurt or harm, then that is evil. If it was done to clear the property so a new building could be built, with the willing consent of the owners, then it could hardly be called evil. It's not merely the act, but the intent behind it which matters.

If a person says, "God told me to sexually abuse and kill young people," that is evil, though the person may also be insane. That sort of action (or any blood sacrifices, be it animal or human) is not condoned by Wiccans. Wiccans also vehemently oppose any sort of physical or sexual abuse of children or adults. Wiccans are generally open about sexuality, but still guard the innocence of their and others' children. Wiccans are commonly more accepting of alternative sexualities and lifestyles, but this absolutely does not include abuse. What happens between consenting adults is their private business. Children are to be properly educated and protected from those who would harm them.

Some might say that Wiccans have a specific Sabbat devoted to death and to understanding that the Dark is a part of the whole cycle of life, death and rebirth. Because of that, some might say that Wiccans worship "the Devil." This is absolutely not so. The Devil (Satan, Old Scratch, and the rest of the names this "demon" goes by) is a Christian fallen angel and the adversary of Jehovah and his son Jesus Christ. Wicca is not a Christian religion, so the notion that Wiccans would worship a Christian Deity (or fallen angel) is erroneous. Most of the traditional trappings of Devil worship were the result of the Inquisition, which created a kind of reverse Christianity. Wicca is trying to resurrect pre-Christian practices and beliefs. Wiccans are respectful of all religions and spiritual paths; this is an integral part of Wiccan training.

REINCARNATION

Some belief in reincarnation is well nigh universal throughout Wicca. What mechanism it takes or what criteria are used differs from individual to individual. Certainly a belief in some sort of soul or spiritual self which lives after the death of the body is universal. An understanding of Karma and cosmic payback for one's actions is also strongly present. With the belief in reincarnation and Karma, the need or existence of a specific heaven or hell is unnecessary. There is a place some believe in, called "the Summerlands," where people go after death to rest between lives, but it is not a place where they will dwell permanently. The idea of Karma eliminates the need for redemption, salvation, or purgatory. People, by their actions or lack thereof, make their own "fate" for future lives, and if they strive to be the best they can and help others, they will eventually not need to return to improve their souls. What happens after that is not really an issue. Most of us have far too much to deal with to realistically contemplate that part of existence.

But Wiccans take responsibility for their actions. They realize that, usually, what the Universe hands them is the result of their actions in the past, and what they may get in the future will be the result of their actions now. There is no shortcut for redemption. It takes hard work, personal responsibility, and a willingness to acknowledge faults to correct or overcome them. Self-examination with the end result of self-betterment is one way a person can "clean up karma" so to speak. It isn't easy, and sometimes is very painful, but is ultimately cleansing. This self-betterment is what is termed The Great Work.

WICCANS AND DEITY

How each individual Wiccan views the universe and interacts with their Gods is a personal choice. There is no set doctrine which mandates certain beliefs or practices with regards to Deity. Apart from the general belief that Deity manifests in both male and female forms, what speculation there is about "Life, the Universe, and Everything," is considered to be just that, speculation, with no definitive "pronouncements from on high."

Some Wiccans are Deistic, believing that a spiritual entity created the universe but that now we are on our own. Some are monologous, believing there is only one Deity, but that it takes many forms and attributes. Some are polytheistic, believing there are many different Gods, each with their own characteristics and areas of influence. Some are Gnostic in outlook and belief, holding that each person is to seek Deity in their own way, and that each person's religious revelations and experiences are true and valid for them. There is no absolute right, true, and singular way to experience Deity or view the universe. Some Wiccans are even agnostic or atheistic. This is very difficult for many non-Wiccans to comprehend. Two people can be Wiccan, they might even be members of the same Coven, and yet the religious practices and beliefs of each may be very different. How one views their Gods or the universe and how each practices worship is a private matter. Occasionally people will inquire, "Which Gods do you worship?" But that is rare.

There are many books published which list Gods and Goddesses and their attributes and characteristics. Wiccans will usually choose a patron Deity, often two—one male and one female. But there are no rules or conventions for choosing, nor do the Deities chosen have to be from the same pantheon. Most Wiccans choose according to an affinity they have for certain Gods, or perhaps they feel they have been chosen by or spoken to by a God or Goddess. However a person feels called, they decide how they want to worship. And there is nothing which restricts a Wiccan to worshipping only two Deities. A person might choose primary Deities, but have affinity for others and include them whenever appropriate.

Wiccans do not worship Satan, nor do they engage in any sort of blood rituals or sacrifice. The fact that Wiccans worship non-Christian Deities may be interpreted by the misguided to mean they worship the Devil, but nothing is farther from the truth. Along with practicing Hindus and Buddhists, who far outnumber Christians in the world, Wiccans are certainly not alone, or even in the minority in their worship of non-Christian deities.

Understanding the variety of worship and the spectrum of Deities is confusing to those new to Wicca. A teacher once told Paul, "My religion is different from your religion. I wouldn't expect you to follow my path; you have to find your own." This confused Paul, until he realized the teacher was talking about which Gods he worshipped and how he worshipped them. Among Wiccans, the fact that each is Wiccan is more important than the fact that one might worship Apollo or another be a follower of Freya.

The immanence of Deity is generally understood by Wiccans. Our Gods are not just up in heaven watching down on us, but manifest in our daily lives. Many Wiccans have a personal relationship with the Gods; they talk to them and can get guidance and instruction. A Wiccan needs no intermediary to talk to the Gods. They are seen as manifest in many small ways, day in and day out, as well as in the grand scheme of things on a cosmic scale.

Most Wiccans believe that Deity manifests in both male and female guises. Some Dianic groups prefer to ignore the male aspect of Deity entirely. Some Wiccans are more Goddess-oriented, some are more God-oriented, and many are strongly dualistic, that is, they believe that one polarity cannot exist without the other. Which Deities any particular Wiccan chooses to worship is entirely up to that individual. Usually one particular patron or pantheon is chosen, though, again, it is up to the individual. The Gods worshipped by Wiccans are, for the most part, not jealous Gods. You can simultaneously worship several, or just one, or even generically (The Goddess and The God). Which Goddess and/or God you worship is your own private business.

Religious Practices

RELIGIOUS TRAINING

Wicca is often criticized for its lack of doctrine. Westerners have been brought up to believe that followers of a religion have uniform beliefs and practices mandated by the religion. If an adherent strays from the specific path, then they are no longer considered a member of the religion. Many Christian denominations started this way. But nowadays Christians are coming together in ecumenical congresses, celebrating shared elements. Wicca is based upon commonalities, and tends to acknowledge but not emphasize the differences between adherents.

Wicca is a "free choice" religion. There is no proselytizing for converts. In fact, many people who really want to join have a hard time finding a group to join! Wicca is for the most part a chosen religious path, the choice being made in adulthood. Few people have been born into the Craft or brought up Wiccan. Most Wiccans consider themselves reformed from whatever religion they were raised in, if any. Children are named and put under the protection of Deity, but are not automatically considered Wiccan or "sealed" into Wicca as with various Christian baptisms. Most Wiccan parents do not expect their children to follow their religious path, but encourage them to explore their own beliefs and make their own decisions. Most Wiccan parents just want their children to grow up to be healthy and well-adjusted and to make their own way without hurting others.

Wiccans have a strong ethic which prohibits taking money for teaching Wicca or for granting Degrees of Initiation. A few Wiccans offer courses and charge for classes, but the majority of Wiccan training is done in small groups at home where no charge is made other than for supplies such as photocopying, candles, and consumables. In this way Wiccan training is very similar to any religious catechism or confirmation course. Learning Wicca is an ongoing process. The first classes may have one of three initiatory Degrees as their end goal, but Wiccans are expected to learn, teach, and study all their lives. Once in Wicca for a few years, they start to develop expertise in various areas, and they continue to study, sometimes teaching others, sometimes being taught. Each individual is unique and has some expertise they can share with others. For example, one can:

- become well-versed in some divinatory system;
- write and perform rituals;
- do research on a specific topic;
- work with herbs, oils, or incense;
- use food and cooking for healing and celebration;
- run a Coven and teach Wicca;
- organize Festivals;
- provide medical services at Festivals or in a Wiccan community.

There is no limitation to how a person can further the Craft.

PRIESTS AND PRIESTESSES

All Initiates are technically Priests and Priestesses. How this plays out in practice differs from group to group. Most Wiccans (with the exception of Dianics) acknowledge Initiations, ceremonies which a person goes through to raise understanding and skill levels. Initiations can be done by others, or by oneself, or by the Gods. If a group does initiations, there are usually three. These are commonly known as the First, Second, and Third Degrees. Because all Wiccan Initiates are considered to be priests, the terms "High Priest" and "High Priestess" are used to designate the people in charge of any given ritual or coven, no matter what their degree level. What training and/or experience is required for each level of Initiation varies widely among the Traditions and paths of Wicca. With Wicca being a religion of priests for the most part, the need for a priest to intercede between a Wiccan and "God" is unnecessary. Most Wiccans have a personal relationship with their Deities.

BOOK OF SHADOWS

In Wicca there is no one sourcebook for the practice and faith. There is no Holy Bible from which all the Wiccan teachings, doctrine, and worship are derived. There is also no one right, true, and only way to be a Wiccan. Wicca is more a Spiritual Path and Way of Life than just a set of teachings and practices

One of the things most all Wiccans have in common is something called a "Book of Shadows." This is an individual's combination note book, journal, memoir, spell book, cookbook, encyclopedia, and general catch-all for information magickal and Wiccan. This term refers to the collection of writings, books, and other materials, written or on disk, which comprise the teachings and practices of that person's Wiccan path and/or Tradition. Rarely is a Book of Shadows limited to only one book. Some of us refer to an "encyclopedia of shadows" or a "bookcase of shadows." This collection can start well before a person actually decides to become Wiccan, or even before they have ever heard of Wicca. Estelle's oldest entries in her Book of Shadows date from her high school days when she made a study of astronomy, and star names and their meanings.

The Book of Shadows most traditionally consists of notes and journals, kept by hand. These writings are in part frequently derived from the accumulated teachings of one's coven or Initiator, plus whatever notes an individual has from lectures and the like. They may also include a journal which details one's magickal workings, listing day, date, and time, perhaps the phase and sign of the Moon, the working attempted, how the working went, and perhaps a listing of results. This is like a scientific notebook of magick. There are also rituals for Sabbats, Esbats, Initiations, and other lore which make up the particular Tradition of the person. This Book of Shadows, as it evolves, becomes the source-book for each Wiccan. Unless a person can afford to buy all the books they want, they usually borrow them and then take notes.

With the explosion of books about Wicca and magick, several Books of Shadows have been published and can be bought off the shelf. There are Wiccan Traditions which have been published and exist whole within the covers of books. Most Wiccans also keep a personal Book of Shadows. For one thing, no published book will have the personal notes and journal of each individual as they study and practice Wicca. And, unless the person is in a strictly traditional group, the Wicca one practices is bound to vary even from the most thorough book. A person might go to a Festival and discover a new ritual, which they just fall in love with and add to their Book of Shadows. It then becomes part of their personal Tradition. Some Traditions mandate that the Book of Shadows be kept secret and shown only to students and fellow initiates, sometimes within just one coven. Some mandate the Book of Shadows must be destroyed upon the owner's death, while others mandate that the Book of Shadows be passed on to a person's successors in the coven.

So just how does a Book of Shadows come into being? The person may take a class. The notes taken in that class become the first entries for a Book of Shadows. If there are readings assigned, notes from the readings are added. If rituals are performed, those are added. If there are Sabbats and Esbats performed, those are also added. Perhaps the person starts a dream journal; that also becomes a part of the Book of Shadows. If one studies the Tarot and keeps notes of teachings or specific readings, those are added. If one goes to a Festival and receives handouts, those go into their Book. If one comes across a recipe for Mooncakes, that is added. A journal of books read, classes attended, Festivals attended, workings done, Sabbats and Esbats attended, all this becomes a part of the Book of Shadows. Personal notes, poetry, writings, musings and the like also are included. Newspaper articles, magazine articles, downloaded information from the Web, and Bulletin Board Service (BBS) transcripts also can be added. In short, anything which can relate to Wicca is included.

Even though a few traditions still maintain all material must be copied by hand, in reality, the personal computer and photocopier have streamlined the process considerably. Before personal desktop publishing, all materials were either handwritten or typed. Because handwriting is so individual and personal, there was the very real threat during more repressive times that Wiccans could be traced through their shared materials. Therefore each Wiccan hand copied the materials, so if caught, no one else would be implicated. Typewriters were never widely used, and carbon paper, mimeo, and ditto were not very permanent records.

Nowadays, all you need is access to a copy machine and a PC, and you can crank out volumes that can be easily duplicated and never really traced back to the source. Xerography provides cheap, clear, and permanent copies, and the three-hole punch, the three-ring notebook, and even plastic page protectors can make for a really first-class Book of Shadows.

All this instant copying does have drawbacks, however. If you hand copy material, you have to process it through your brain while you copy. This ensures that the material will be fully read at least once. And the process of copying the Books of another usually ensures personal contact, as most Wiccans will never lend out their Book of Shadows. This can then lead to questions and discussion about the material being copied, and the student thereby gets more information and the training progresses. So the old ways had more reasons behind them than just keeping people safe. It was a way to pass along information and ensure comprehension. Just because a person receives a photocopied handout does not guarantee that he or she will either read it or understand it.

Incidental material which may find its way into a Book of Shadows includes: recipes, songs, newspaper or magazine articles, personal correspondence (including e-mail printouts), astrological charts, photocopies of rare old books, and price lists and addresses of places one can buy herbs, jewelry, books, and magickal paraphernalia. One thing it should *not* include are the names, addresses, and phone numbers of fellow Wiccans, especially not lists which correlate Craft names with mundane names or addresses or phone numbers. A mundane name is the regular everyday name a person uses in the non-Wiccan world, the one which would be in the phone book. It's usually the one given at birth by one's parents. They are usually included in one's personal address book, but not identified as Wiccan. Craft names are usually remembered. If the people you know are Out, this might not be a big issue, but not all Wiccans are Out, so they are very reluctant to have their names or telephone number and/or address given out with specifically Wiccan material.

Being Out is a term which refers to a Wiccan's openness to the rest of society about their religious beliefs. Many Wiccans are not Out, that is when directly questioned about their religion they will answer with a portion of the truth but will not directly state "I am Wiccan." Other Wiccans are definitely Out and may even make a point of stating "I am Wiccan" to any and all who will listen. There are also many shades of being Out, from "in the broom closet" to totally open.

With respect to Craft names, most Wiccans do adopt a Craft name which is used with others and in coven or Wiccan settings. It is not at all uncommon to have very close friends whose real names you do not know, because you only relate to them in a Wiccan context. You may also not know their addresses or telephone numbers, let alone where they work. This can be a drawback, but it can also protect people if they are not Out or feel their Wiccan affiliations might cause them trouble at work or elsewhere. Craft names are usually used and memorized, and not written down, especially where they would be easily accessible to people who might use them in unfriendly ways. Some Wiccans have been barraged with phone calls and witnessing by "well-meaning" Christians who want to "save" them, when such information has leaked out. People have also received hate mail and other more unsettling communications. Especially when communicating by e-mail, BBS, or internet, it is vital that names or handles not be associated with telephone numbers or addresses or mundane names.

ETHICS

Ethics are very important in Wicca, because of the personal responsibility each Wiccan is expected to hold. Each person must form their own ethical belief system and do their best to adhere to it. The Wiccan Rede, Law of Three, and Golden Rule help set some guidelines, but as the modern world is full of compromises and contradictions, each person must think actively about which compromises and contradictions are acceptable and which are not. Ethics can change, evolve, and grow over time. Other religions have a ready-made ethical code and rules which adherents are expected to abide by, though the interpretations may differ from sect to sect. Wiccans, on the other hand, have few. Each Wiccan builds his or her own. In practice there are many areas where most Wiccans tend to agree. The active exploration of ethics and values is ongoing throughout a Wiccan's life. It is an integral part of the Great Work which results in self-betterment.

CONFIDENTIALITY

Confidentiality is a crucial ethical principle among Wiccans. Our religion stresses secrecy as a safety measure, for in the past Witches were persecuted and occasionally put to death for their beliefs and practices. This happens even occasionally today, though to a much lesser degree.

Confidentiality means never exposing another Wiccan's identity or affiliation to anyone.

Confidentiality also is important for keeping Craft Secrets, to ensure that certain practices and techniques do not fall into untrained, unprepared hands.

Most Traditions have oaths of secrecy which initiates must swear to: keep the secrets within the group, do not reveal the identities of one's coven-mates, where and when the coven meets, and the like. Most Wiccans are not Out, preferring to keep their religion a personal, private matter. There are real, frequently justified fears that a person's Wiccan affiliation could cost them their job, home, friendships, marriage, children or other important real-world possessions or affiliations. Because of this, Wiccans tend to view themselves as a persecuted minority. Certainly some Christian sects would like to convert all the Witches to their brand of Christianity, and generally there is still a great deal of misunderstanding and many misconceptions about Wicca, Wiccans, and Witches.

In an attempt to counteract some of this perceived persecution, some Wiccans readily adopt the term "Witch" to describe themselves. Others take longer to adopt the "W" word. A few never adopt it. The word "Witch" has certain connotations in this culture which Wiccans are trying to overcome and dispel. To this end, a few Wiccans have taken an "in-your-face" attitude with respect to being a Witch and practicing Wicca. But most Wiccans are just plain people who have a home, job, spouse, and kids and also happen to be Wiccan.

With the persecuted minority issue comes the issue of teaching minors about the Craft. Most Wiccan training groups will not accept people under eighteen, because the teachers fear prosecution by an irate parent, grandparent, or school teacher. Those who *will* teach minors usually require a parental consent form. Wiccans who have minor children may teach them about the Craft, but they are also careful to make sure that their children will not casually talk about what they are learning. Well-meaning school teachers have tried (and occasionally succeeded) to get children taken away from parents, believing the parent was teaching the children about "demon worship." In some areas of the country, parents may choose to keep their religious interests secret even from their children until the children are old enough to understand and abide by the secrecy which may be necessary. Each family makes these decisions for itself, and Wiccans respect the decisions each family makes.

The perception of being a persecuted minority, and the threat of exposure, can make some Wiccans paranoid. The average Wiccan is highly cautious about discussing with "non-Pagans" matters pertaining to the Craft, and will think carefully before opening up to persons who might not be fully aware of what Wicca is. Some people carry this caution to extremes, never breathing a word about Wicca to anyone except within their own coven. When asked what they did the previous night, most practitioners will not answer, "We celebrated Samhain." They might say instead, "I was at a church function" or "I was at a party with a few close friends" or "I was at a family gathering." All of which is true, of course, depending upon your perspective. Being "low key" about their beliefs is the way most Wiccans operate if they are not Out.

Wiccan Culture

The ideals and values that Wiccans pursue at times run directly counter to the consumer-oriented, keeping-up-with-the-Joneses, more-is-good, progress-is-desirable, we-own-the-Earth mindsets of the mainstream culture. "Renew, reuse, recycle" is a mantra understood and practiced by most Wiccans. The pursuit of riches for its own sake is considered illogical, though most Wiccans have a regular nine-to-five real world job to pay the bills and provide the resources to practice their chosen life style. Many Wiccans would happily do Wicca full-time if they could manage it, even if the money was less, for they would be doing what makes them happy. While there are a number of Wiccans who have managed to go back to the land and are working towards self-sufficiency, most Wiccans are urban Pagans. They try to honor and work within the Cycle of the Seasons rather than try to dominate or conquer the natural cycles. Most of the average things which "push the buttons" of people today hold little fascination for Wiccans. Wiccans tend to socialize together and stay within their own groups simply because they all share similar values and mindsets. Mundane is the term used to describe things or people non-Wiccan or non-Pagan, and for those in the culture of Wicca the term is very specific. This gives the impression to outsiders that Wiccans are cliquish or elitist or even closed, but this isn't necessarily so. Rather, Wiccans have a specific culture they want to pursue without outside interference. Once a new person passes the initial screening to guarantee similar interests and mindset, they are usually welcomed with open arms into the fold.

COMMON VALUES
Respect for the Earth Mother

Ecology, recycling, walking gently on the Earth, and trying to reuse, renew, and recycle are all widely adopted practices. Self-sufficiency is an ideal, but few attain it. Generally, Wiccans do what they can in their own way to contribute to making the world a better place than when they came along. At Festivals, Pagans and Wiccans regularly clean up and cheerfully remove whatever was left behind by the previous group. The site is usually in better shape afterwards (although at home most Wiccans are notoriously sloppy housekeepers). Wiccans believe that we do not own the Earth, nor are we the masters of the Earth, nor was the Earth given us to use, exploit, or destroy as we want. This is our home, and we live here, but nobody can really own the Earth or any part of it. That notion of ownership of land is just a societal convention. Wiccans believe that we are stewards of the Earth, and will work to keep it clean and well-managed, and as unspoiled as possible. This can range from participating in a Save-the-Rainforests campaign; to choosing not to have a conventional yard, but rather to let natural animals and plants be in the space; to composting and not using chemical fertilizers or pesticides; to not building a new home but rather renovating an existing home; to refusing to use certain products or support certain industries which pollute or exploit the Earth and/or its peoples. There is a strong respect for life—all life, not just human life or the life of certain privileged humans. But quality of life is also honored. Most Wiccans are strongly pro-choice, and that includes the absolute right to choose to *not* have an abortion as well as have one, if that is the option which causes the least harm.

Wicca is a nature-oriented religion, so Wiccans are aware of the seasons and how the world changes as the years progress. There is a simultaneous understanding of the endless cycle of the seasons, and yet also the uniqueness of each day as it comes and goes. There is also some mindfulness of the longer cycles of time, and how what we do today has an impact upon what others may or may not be able to do tomorrow or decades or centuries from now.

Equality

Belief in the Equality of the Sexes and Races is fairly universal among Wiccans. Some groups may choose to be open to only one sex or those practicing a certain lifestyle choice, but that does not mean others are denigrated. It just means that this group is working on that particular Path. People are generally taken as they are and are not judged by their skin color, size, ability, background, or education. Sexual preference is a matter of personal choice, and as long as a person harms no one, s/he is free to practice with other consenting adults. Violence is not tolerated, and abuse is considered something to be eliminated from all families and other groups. Children are valued and encouraged to be as free as possible to learn and grow within the guidelines of a loving family structure, whatever that may be.

Education

Education, reading, and general intellectual pursuits are valued highly. Festivals and Gatherings strongly emphasize teaching and workshipping. Wiccan training includes reading, discussion, experiential learning, and research. The average Wiccan reads numerous books every month, usually several books at a time. Many Wiccans are either actively writing a book, or have ideas for several books they are planning to get to when they have the time. Authors are often featured guests at Festivals and Gatherings. As Wicca has been primarily spread through the printed word over the decades since its revival, this obsession with books, education, reading, and learning is understandable. Formal education is considered nice, but there is little intellectual snobbery. Being self-taught is as valid as a university degree, provided you know your stuff. With all this emphasis on reading, there is relatively little time for TV or other popular cultural pursuits. However, having a computer is becoming more and more important, as is being hooked up to the Internet. There has been no concrete survey, but some authors estimate that 60 to 75% of all Wiccans are currently on the Internet. The proliferation of Web sites dedicated to Pagan and Wiccan topics attests to this. The drawback is that being on the Web will take up as much time as you are willing to give it, and can become an empty pursuit, if not carefully monitored.

GROUP ORGANIZATION

Wiccans are usually proud and frequently vocal about being anarchistic and "anti-hierarchical." While you can argue that the term "organized Wicca" may be somewhat of an oxymoron, Wiccans, like all human beings, have developed their own systems of organization, hierarchies and pecking orders. Though most non-Wiccans may find our organizations unfamiliar and possibly confusing, the systems that we work with are pretty simple.

The Coven

The coven is the basic small-group structure of Wicca. As a

religion, there are certainly larger, organized Wiccan "churches" with even hundreds of people in rare instances, but most Wiccans still meet and interact within their own covens at home. A coven is a group of Wiccan people who have come together to work magick and to study Wicca and other related things. In many ways a coven can be likened to a Bible study group. People meet, usually at a private home to read materials and discuss and study Wicca as a religion and as a life path.

Traditionally, it is said, a coven always contained thirteen members, but modern covens can be as large or as small as the members want. The internal hierarchy, rules, and operations of a coven are strictly up to the members involved. Covens are formed for many reasons. Teaching or Training Covens train new people. Working Covens are groups of initiates who meet to work magick and study Wicca and related topics. Covens can also be subsets of various denominations of Wicca; a Gardnerian Coven would be a local branch of a larger lineage of Gardnerian Wicca.

The modern Wiccan Coven usually consists of three to ten people who meet weekly, though this can vary widely. Traditionally, a coven is headed by a High Priestess (HPS) and a High Priest (HP), though this is not mandatory. If a person is lucky enough to be able to join a Working Coven as a student, they will probably receive training and get a wonderful Wiccan education. Many covens have been started by a few friends who have read about Wicca and, finding nobody who could teach them, have decided to get together and do things on their own. Thirteen was traditionally the maximum membership of a coven, because thirteen people are few enough to interact easily on a personal level and yet factions remain a large enough percentage of the group to make secret activities very difficult. Also, getting many more people together requires renting a hall, as most living rooms are pretty crowded even with thirteen people.

A document, detailing the rules and regulations of being a member and running the coven may be drawn up. This document is known as a covenant. A covenant can be as simple as one or two lines, or it can be as elaborate as the U.S. Constitution. Generally, only long-running, well-established covens require a written covenant; verbal discussions are the standard. The group does need to make a few joint decisions though. For instance:

- What are the purposes and goals of our meetings (teaching, working, research, magick...etc.)?
- Are we going to be an Eclectic group, or tied to a certain Tradition?
- Is our membership closed or open?

There are also decisions to be made regarding internal organization:

- Will there be a specific HPS and HP in charge?
- Will new members be admitted by majority vote? (Is black-balling allowed?)
- Is the coven to be secret or open?
- When and how often will the group meet?
- Will the coven have a group Altar, Sacred Space, Temple, Tools, Books and the like?
- Where will the group meet?

The place that the Coven most commonly meets is traditionally called the Covenstead, usually a private home (but not necessarily that of the HPS or HP). Frequently it is the place with the most room, or where the group can keep their stuff.

Sometimes Wiccans start meeting, and only after a time realize they are actually a coven. Sometimes the organizational discussions come only after problems develop within the group.

Creating New Covens

Interpersonal conflicts occur among Wiccans as among everyone else. Conflict is a part of human interaction. A Wiccan tradition called "hiving off," allows for disaffected people in a coven to leave and start their own new independent coven. There are many reasons for a new coven to hive off, among them:

- The original coven gets too big.
- People move away and are unable to continue meeting with the original coven.
- People become dissatisfied and leave.
- People are asked to leave a coven and go off and start their own.
- People may want to try something new and different, and the old coven is just not interested in changing.

As you can see, hiving off is a mechanism for allowing disagreement without having it turn into acrimony or hard feelings. But the tradition is that once a coven had hived off of a parent coven, the daughter coven is independent and there is usually no mixing of memberships. Generally, you must choose one coven over the other. This also varies from Tradition to Tradition. There is, for instance, in some Traditions the custom of the "Witch Queen," in which the HPS of the parent coven is recognized as sort of a "senior" High Priestess by the HPS's of any daughter covens. This custom sometimes helps when there are inter-coven disputes.

Wiccan tradition states that a person can only belong to one coven at a time. This is to prevent divided loyalties, but also to prevent group hopping. This may seem restrictive, and some Wiccans have modified the rule to mean one coven of a type. In other words, a person may head up a Teaching Coven, and be a member of a separate Working Coven as well. Or one might be a member of a coven that puts on regular large-group rituals and a more secretive ceremonial magick coven as well. In this case, covens become more like small organizations than tightly-knit groups of compatriots. Most of the long-established Wiccan Traditions have their own specific rules regarding coven membership.

Like Wicca itself, your coven becomes what you make of it. As an example, the authors are members of a small, highly eclectic, and anti-hierarchical Working Coven. Who is in charge depends upon who is leading the unit at the time. Whoever is doing the Sabbat is in charge for that Sabbat. Additionally, Estelle is co-head of a separate Teaching Coven which meets for a year-and-a-day, providing a Wiccan First Degree initiation. Paul participates as a guest speaker on occasion.

Paul is a member of a national-level Wiccan Coven that helps provide security at Festivals and Gatherings throughout the United States. Estelle is not a member of this group, though she has helped out on occasion. Both Estelle and Paul are members of a local Wiccan Church with tax-exempt status, and Paul holds ministerial credentials through that church. Estelle considers herself a member of two covens (the Working group and the Teaching group), but as each has different purposes, she sees no conflict between the two. Paul is officially a member of only one coven (the security group), though he is active in several other Wiccan groups. The Wiccan Church they belong to is not a coven (it says so in its bylaws), though it provides an umbrella structure for members to get federal recognition and protections for their separate covens if they wish.

There are very few hard-and-fast rules. A coven is what you make of it, and it grows and evolves and changes over time. Some covens are reputed to have been in existence for centuries. Some can be documented for several decades. Some, like Estelle's Teaching Coven, are meant to exist for only a specific period.

Traditions or Lineages

A "Tradition" or "Lineage" is a group of covens which all trace their descent from a single group or person, and follow basically the same tenets, teachings, and practices. How large any specific Tradition might be varies widely. There are estimates of about 20,000 Gardnerians throughout the world. Other Traditions may be no larger than a single coven.

Traditions spread in various ways. They can grow through the hiving off process. Or people might come to a certain place, or covenstead, to get the training and carry the teaching back to their homes. Some Traditions derive from other Traditions (Seax Wicca, for example, is an off-shoot of Gardnerian Wicca). Some derive from older Fam-Trads and have been modified and changed so outsiders may enter. The original Fam-Trad may still exist, but the derivation has grown well beyond the original. A Tradition may be created by a person publishing a book (like Starhawkian Wicca) and grow as more people read the book and adopt that way of doing things.

Churches and Clergy

Actual Wiccan Churches do exist. There are a number, in several states, which have organized and gone to the trouble of gaining state and/or federal recognition and tax-exempt status. These groups are usually small (under 50 people) and rarely own land or buildings. Even tax-exempt groups for the most part meet in people's homes. Some groups rent space for Sabbats and other large celebrations, but the bulk of group business is conducted in homes. These churches are usually loose groups of people and may or may not be of one single Tradition. Others are "umbrella organizations," which allow members to practice as they choose yet gain state and federal recognition and status. Most Wiccan churches hold Sabbats in a regular place. Individual members are encouraged to hold Sabbats in their own covens as well.

Once registered, these groups can "ordain" ministers who are empowered to perform weddings and generally enjoy the rights and privileges of any other recognized clergy. It is becoming increasingly important to Wiccans to have their own clergy to legally perform weddings, officiate at the namings of children (similar to a Christian christening), minister to Wiccans in prison and in hospitals, conduct memorial services, and provide all the other services and support which clergy offer.

Though many people hold ministerial credentials through a Wiccan church or other organization—the Universal Life Church and the Unitarians are also popular—there are few if any paid clergy within Wicca in the U.S. today. Due to the nature of the religion and the structure of Wicca, it is rare for a congregation of Wiccans to be sizable enough to support full-time professional clergy.

Wicca resembles the Quakers, the Jehovah's Witnesses, the Mormons, and many other Christian denominations which survive well without a professional clerical body.

Ordained Wiccan ministers usually offer their services in the context of their everyday lives, which generally includes a regular job. The ratio of registered ministers to parishioners in Wicca may be higher than in the mainstream Christian population. Each coven may not have a minister, but generally there is at least one Wiccan clergy person in any sizable city throughout most of the United States.

Wiccan ministers are popular among people who are spiritual, but do not belong to a specific church or ascribe to a specific faith or creed. Paul has conducted more weddings for non-Wiccans than for Wiccans. The clergy of most mainstream faiths require a person to be a member of their church, or at least to be of a compatible faith, to marry them. Wicca, on the other hand, is a religion which has little set faith or dogma, so there is less conflict with differing beliefs. And because of the diversity of beliefs within Wicca, most Wiccan clergy are able to operate in many different creeds and work with differing ceremonial structures and formats, according to who is being served. This is not a special part of Wiccan clerical training, it is just a natural expression of the way Wicca is.

Other Organizations

Because of the structure of Wicca—based on small groups, generally the size of an extended family, possibly linked by ties and/or Tradition—Wicca is more like a network or a web than a congregation or a community. Wiccans have friends who are Wiccan, and they might socialize together and even possibly meet at open Sabbats in a particular area, but there are few, if any, larger organizations of Wiccans anywhere. Groups that have members nationwide are still usually based on the coven model and operate as a loose confederation of local covens. There may or may not be an annual meeting of members or representatives. It is quite common to have Wiccan friends you see regularly at Festivals and yet not know their mailing address, full legal name, where they live, what they do for a living, or even their phone number. Most Wiccans use "Craft names" within Wicca; that is, they chose a name for themselves. It is quite common to have Wiccan friends whom you know well, but only by their Craft names, and whom you have no idea how to contact outside a Festival.

FESTIVALS (GATHERINGS)

At Festivals and gatherings, Wiccans from all over meet, share teaching and ideas, and celebrate being Wiccan. Festivals started out as a sort of Wiccan version of church camp. People would gather at an outdoor site, camp, and hang out together for a weekend or a week. As the years have gone by, outdoor Festivals still thrive, but nowadays there are almost as many indoor Festivals. These resemble conventions or trade shows.

Festivals have become the Pagan melting pot in the United States. At a Festival you can meet Gardnerians, Dianics, and all sorts of Wiccans in between, as well as people of many other Pagan Paths. This was the first venue at which people of different Wiccan Traditions could meet and talk and get a chance to see "how the others did it." Many Pagans plan their vacations around these Festivals, which now take place year-round.

All Festivals are heavily education-oriented. The standard Festival, whether it be a weekend or week long (or longer), starts with some sort of opening ritual followed by many workshops, lectures, and demonstrations. Authors come to talk about and sell their books. People vie for the privilege of hosting an evening group ritual and help with the staffing duties that allow the Festival to run smoothly. People specialize in safety, gatekeeping, cooking, administration, first aid, psychological centering, child care, or other necessary duties. Typically, there are three to five or more workshop periods in a Festival day with a break for lunch, and then some sort of communal supper followed by an evening ritual or entertainment. Drumming and dancing carry well into the night, and the whole process starts again the next morning.

Most Festivals are family oriented, and children are welcome. The Festival is the time to catch up with friends on news, meet new people, trade stories and tips, and generally relax in a very Pagan-friendly atmosphere. And because some of the same people return year after year, most Festivals have evolved their own individualistic styles, with almost a life and identity of their own. One might be mainly focused on partying, while another is more concerned with exploring certain specific issues.

At most typical Festivals something known as "Pagan Space" is created. This is a community gestalt which arises out of many Pagans living together and interacting without outsiders present. Most Pagans never experience such a feeling except at a Festival. For once, we are not a minority. The atmosphere is relaxed and people can speak freely about most any topic of interest and find willing participants to converse with.

Many outdoor Festivals are clothing optional, or at least have an area where one can go without clothing if that is desired. For Pagans, nudity is just another clothing option, not exhibitionistic or prurient in nature.

Nudity is an issue for Wiccans because it touches upon so many cultural paradigms which Wiccans want to change. The issue of the best, proper or correct body shape, size, color, or type is laid to rest when all are nude and it can be observed there is nobody with a perfect body. Clothing as a mark of status and wealth is eliminated when all are nude. Nudity can also be a way of breaking down personal inhibitions, not as a prelude to sex, but as a low-ering of defensive barriers in a creation of a group mind, preparatory to doing magick. Clothing can interfere with magickal energy, and most all Wiccan Initiations are per-formed with the Initiate nude. Partial or nearly total nudi-ty has been a clothing norm in many societies, past and present, and most of those societies were Pagan. One of the first things the Christian Missionaries did to the "primi-tive" tribespeople they converted was to make them wear clothing. So having nudity as another clothing option can be another way Wiccans have of consciously changing the Christian mindsets they may have been raised with. How one reacts to nudity can also be a way in which Wiccans tell who is "one of us" and who is not.

Festivals also usually include a "Merchant's Row," an area where people set up their wares for sale to the partici-pants. Most Wiccans do their holiday and ritual tool shop-ping here, no matter what time of the year the Festival takes place. The merchants display a great assortment of wares, from handmade to commercial, but all of interest to the average Wiccan.

The Festivals and Gatherings are the closest you can get to an actual Wiccan Community.

THE INTERNET

Internet communication is fast becoming popular within Wicca. The Internet lends itself readily to Wiccan communication, and many Wiccans are comfortable working in "virtual reality." If a person is a solitaire (that is practicing Wicca by themselves or with only a couple of close friends), the Internet can be their only contact with the wider Wiccan community outside of books. And virtual reality is the only real-world construct where mundanes (non-Wiccans) can experience the "time without a time and a place without a place" phenomenon which is created while in a Circle. All you need to know is an e-mail address and you are in touch with whomever. You can chat in real time on BBSs. There are many Wiccan/Pagan boards, usually under the larger category of alt.religion, either Wiccan or Pagan. More commonly, people just leave messages and have a conversation over days and weeks, each person reading and replying at leisure. People can easily retain their anonymity and speak as freely as they want, but it is wise to follow the conventions of polite BBS communication.

Also remember that Internet communication, though it feels like conversation, is still written and therefore possibly permanent. People have gone off on certain topics without either reviewing or thinking twice about what they are saying, or the way they are saying it, and these ideas and expressions have returned at a later date to haunt them. It is wise to err on the side of being polite and circumspect.

Privacy on the Internet is an important issue. Internet communication uses handles, and one should be careful not to have names or addresses or phone numbers associated with handles. People unfriendly to Wicca have been known to intercept such information and use it to either proselytize or intimidate. Keep in mind that most Internet communications are not confidential; you should be able to anticipate problems before they happen.

The Wheel of the Year

There are eight major Wiccan holidays that make up the wheel of the year. These eight Sabbats or solar holy days occur at roughly six-and-a-half-week intervals throughout the calendar year. They have evolved from several Traditions. They are seasonal, and reflect the growing cycle in both agrarian and hunting societies. Mythologically, they represent the yearly cycle of the Maiden, Mother, and Crone of the Goddess, and the birth, marriage, maturation, and death of the God.

The new and full moons—twelve or thirteen of each during the year—are the Esbats or lunar holy days. A Wiccan can also worship every week, though there is no standard day of the week set aside for worship.

THE SABBATS

Samhain, October 31 (also called Halloween, All Hallows Eve, Hallowmass, Day of the Dead). Samhain (pronounced *sow-enn*) has come to be known as the "Witches' New Year," so we will start with Samhain, though the Wheel is cyclical and ever turning, without a definitive starting point. This holiday is one of the most important and revered in the Wiccan calendar. In an agrarian society, this is the time of year (depending on the local climate) when farmers culled the herds, slaughtering the excess livestock and saving the best breeding stock. It is therefore occasionally also called the Blood Harvest. The grain harvest was in, and farmers were able to accurately assess how many animals they could reasonably feed through the winter. They also knew how many people they could feed. The frost had come, and winter was coming, so the meat would stay fresh longer in nature's "refrigerator." In hunting societies, the "Wild Hunt" was abroad, and the tribe was more dependent upon their hunters for food, as the plants were becoming dormant for the winter.

This holiday marks the time when the souls of all who have died throughout the year pass over to the other side, and all the souls of those who will be born in the next year come into our world. Celebrations are oriented toward mourning and letting go of those who have died, especially those who have died in the past year. There is also a general remembrance of ancestors who have come before, with the telling of the family stories, personal histories, and coven lore. This is the time of the year when "the veil between the worlds is thinnest." Magick can be very strong and extremely effective.

A common practice at Samhain is the "dumb supper." This is a meal which is shared with those who have gone before. An extra plate is set and filled with food for those who are no longer with us. After the meal, this food is usually set outside for whatever creatures happen along; Wiccans try not to waste. This dumb supper is a meal when nobody speaks, the time instead being used to reflect upon those who have gone before. Traditionally, "Dumb" referred to those who could not speak (i.e., your ancestors), not the silent diners at the meal. But as Wicca is an evolving religion, this silent meal has come to have a modern interpretation of this tradition. The Samhain Feast may frequently consist of the root crops, also the last fruits of the harvest, as well as many meat and game dishes. Some Wiccans eat meat only at Samhain.

Mythologically, this holiday is when the Goddess mourns her slain consort, the God, and she contemplates the coming birth of her child by him. The Goddess is also honored in her Crone aspect. This holiday also mythically celebrates the death of the God, as he lays down his life for the community, or as the God of the Wild Hunt, symbolizing the animals hunted for food.

Yule, December 21st (also called Winter Solstice). Yule is the holiday which was transmuted into Christmas (Christ's actual birth has variously been calculated to have been in the springtime, nearer the Spring Equinox or in March). This is the time of the year when winter is full upon the land. It is a time of leisure, storytelling, and sharing skills and traditions. It is the longest night, and Wiccan traditions include burning the Yule Log, which is lit before the Sun goes down and tended all night until the Sun comes up the next morning. Many Wiccan groups meet and greet the Sunrise after this longest night. Yule trees are a Pagan tradition and are decorated each year. The Yule feast includes many of the traditional "Christmas foods," including cookies and candy and hearty roasts or stews. Presents are exchanged over the days starting at Yule and continuing through Twelfth Night (January 6th). Twelfth Night is an official Christian Holiday, also known as "Little Christmas," which started in the Middle Ages and falls on the twelfth day after Christmas. Wiccans celebrate Twelfth Night, and keep the traditional Christian Date of January 6th. It gives us a few more days to catch up on the sales.

Mythologically, the Goddess gives birth to the Sun God on the longest night, and Wiccans celebrate the birth (or rebirth) of the Sun God. Some Wiccan groups have Mother Bertha come and pass out presents. Mother Bertha is a Crone who gives presents, and sometimes steals children, if they are bad. Some Traditions see this as a God day in the middle of the Goddess (dark) time of the year.

Candlemas, February 1st or 2nd [also called Imbolc, Immilch, Brigid's Day or Bride (pronounced *breed*)]. Candlemas is the time when winter is still on the land, but spring is coming. In earlier agricultural societies, this was the break point; you either had enough food to last until the first spring plants came up, or you didn't. If you did, it was a time to celebrate. If you didn't, it was still a time to have a party with what was left, so not to prolong the starvation. It is also the time when it is readily apparent that the days are lengthening, and the time of the long, dark nights is ending. It is also usually the coldest time of the year, so survival is a big issue, even with the coming of spring. Wiccans celebrate with a bonfire and a blessing of the tools. In some agrarian societies, it was the time when the planting and plowing tools were brought out and readied for the planting in the spring. It was called Brigid's Day, because Brigid is a Goddess of the forge, and she would bless their tools. Nowadays, Wiccans use a number of tools, and the blessing of the tools brings a fertility of ideas as well as fertility of the soil. In other societies (depending on location), this was the time of the birth of the new lambs, thus it is called Immilch or the time of new milk.

Mythologically, the Goddess has recovered from the birth of her child, and the child has lived and gotten strong so he will survive. Imbolc can also be a time of Dedication and Initiation. Some see this as the time when the Goddess is renewed as Maiden after the birth of her child.

Oestarra, March 21st (also known as Spring Equinox, Eostre). Oestarra is one of the two holidays which may or may not be celebrated by Wiccans. Some Traditions do not celebrate Oestarra or Mabon. This holiday may or may not correspond with spring, depending upon where you live. It is a time to celebrate spring (or the coming spring) and fertility and get things ready for the coming growing season. In most places there has been a significant thaw, and even if the earth still has snow, it is becoming obvious that winter will end soon. Wiccans celebrate with painting eggs and celebrating fertility. It is a day of balance, when day and night are of equal length.

Mythologically, some Traditions celebrate the change from the Goddess half or dark half of the year to the God half or light half. If it is spring, a feast of asparagus, new greens, and other spring plants is appropriate. The Goddess has changed from Crone to Maiden, and she is a young girl ready to grow with her son/consort as the year grows. The Sun God is growing fast and is a vital and healthy child.

Beltane, April 30 or May 1 (also known as May Eve, Walpurgisnacht, Bealtain). Beltane is the second biggest holiday in the Wiccan calendar. It is a fertility festival.

Mythologically, the Goddess and God achieve puberty and become sexually aware. Beltane celebrates their wedding, and the Goddess—in mating with the God—changes from Maiden to Mother. It is also the time of spring and the planting of the crops. Animals come into season and mate. In agricultural societies, the fields were blessed and occasionally couples went out into the fields and made love to help renew the fertility of the soil. In hunting societies the emphasis changed from hunting to gathering as the main source of food for the group.

Wiccans frequently celebrate with a feast of spring plants, asparagus, new greens, and other early plants. Usually fresh flowers are brought to celebrate the new growing season. There can be a Beltane Lottery, by which a "May Queen" and "Green Man" are chosen, and they become the living representatives of the Goddess and God for the community. People serve as May Queen and Green Man sometimes for the day, sometimes for longer, depending upon the group's traditions and customs. In some groups these people act as spiritual advisors for the time they serve. They may prophesy for group members. They might give guidance to the group as a whole or to individuals. This office is considered sacred and usually is open to Initiates only. May baskets may be exchanged with wishes for fertility and a prosperous summer. Beltane is a happy time; spring is here, summer is coming, and we all can see the abundance and gifts of the Goddess and God. The outdoor Festival season unofficially starts.

Midsummer, June 21st (also known as Litha or Summer Solstice) is the longest day of the year. The crops and gardens are planted. We are starting to get the first fruits of our plantings. Life is easy and good. Days are warm and long, winter is only a memory.

Mythologically, the Goddess is pregnant by the God, and her belly swells with new life. In farming societies this was the time for celebration between planting and harvest. In hunting societies, the hunters made new weapons and traveled to get the supplies they needed for successful hunting in the winter.

This is the prime time for vacations and Festivals. Wiccans celebrate with a feast of strawberries and other fruits and greens. It is a time to get together, visit, and relax. It is the longest day, but we are also aware that now the nights get longer, and that winter will come again. Some Traditions consider this to be a Goddess day in the middle of the God time of the year. The Goddess as Mother is in her glory.

Lughnasadh, August 1st (also known as Lammas). Lughnasadh celebrates the first fruits of the harvest, so a big feast is part of the sacred rites, often with a corn dolly or other homemade breads. is the celebration of the first harvest. The Summer fruits are ripening and our gardens are yielding many wonderful things. The days are getting shorter, and we are very aware that winter will come.

Mythologically, some Traditions see this as the time of the Death of the God, a willing sacrifice to allow the community to continue. Though the God may die, the Goddess is with child and the family will continue. A feast of grains, fruits, and vegetables is celebrated. Where this is the time of the main grain harvest, the God is in his guise as John Barleycorn, the Grain God. In hunting societies, the boys were initiated at this time of the year into the mysteries of hunting, and they prepared to take part in the hunting over the winter to come. There were contests and games designed to test and improve hunting skills. Therefore, some groups also hold Lughnasadh games, contests of athletics for the young to show their prowess and for the old to enjoy their skill and cunning. Other Traditions see this time as the God's time when he can display his prowess and strength for all to admire.

Mabon, September 21st (also known as Autumnal Equinox). Mabon is the other day of balance, of equal length of day and night. It can symbolize the change from the God or light time of the year to the Goddess or dark time of the year. This is the time of the grain harvest in some areas, and so the Death of the God can be celebrated at this Sabbat as well. This is also the period of highest energy within the animal kingdom, as many wild species come into rut, while others are busy preparing for their winter hibernations

Mythologically, the death of the God is a willing sacrifice, the God in his prime who willingly lays down his life so his people may live and grow. In hunting societies with plants dying and gathering ending, hunting began in earnest.

Wiccans celebrate with a feast of grains, fruits, and vegetables, especially the first apples. This is also the time of the main harvest, and Wiccans will offer the first and best fruits to the Gods as thanks for the fertility which they have granted to their People. The harvest is celebrated and the abundance is stored for the coming winter. The Goddess is pregnant, yet also a widow.

The next Sabbat is Samhain, and so the wheel has turned yet again. Wiccans see the year as a cycle, ever-changing and never-ending. Sometimes, celebrating the Sabbats is referred to as "Turning the Wheel," implying the seasons will only progress if we help the cycle along. There are several cycles imposed represented in the year:

• the Goddess/God cycle (light and dark times);
• the cycle of Goddess as she progresses from Maiden to Mother to Crone, and through renewal/rebirth back to Maiden;
• the cycle of the life of the God from birth through marriage and maturity to death and rebirth;
• the cycle of the growing year;
• the cycle of the hunting/gathering year.

Different Traditions honor different cycles. And the seasons are different in various parts of the country. So

Wiccans change and adapt the Sabbats to their needs as they see fit in their lives and localities.

THE ESBATS

The Lunar cycle gives rise to the Esbats, celebrations which are based on the Lunar month. Esbats are seen as mainly Goddess-oriented. The New Moon symbolizes the Maiden, and as she waxes, she changes from Maiden to Mother. At Full Moon the Goddess is at her greatest power and fertility. Sometimes the full moon symbolizes the pregnant Goddess. As the Moon Wanes, the Goddess changes from Mother to Crone until she "dies" (or goes into seclusion) each month at the Dark of the Moon (the Moon's Fourth Face) and is reborn as Maiden when the Moon is new again. This Lunar cycle is also seen as a celebration of a woman's menstrual cycle, the time of actual menstruation being the time of the dark of the Moon when she goes into seclusion. Wiccans may celebrate Esbats at Full Moons only, at both New and Full Moons, or at each quarter, roughly every seven days. In feminist Dianic Wiccan groups, Esbats are more important than the Sabbats.

The Full Moon is the time for the ceremony known as "Drawing Down the Moon" into the High Priestess. This is a rite when the Goddess is made manifest in her Priestess, and the Priestess may prophesy, offer advice, and/or give counsel to Her Coven members. Below is a copy of "The Charge of the Goddess," which refers to the full moon ceremony and is possibly the one document that is common to most Wiccan groups. The original version and inspiration comes from the books *The Golden Ass* by Apuliaus and also *Aradia or the Gospel of the Witches* by Leyland. Dion Fortune re-wrote and expanded it. Gardner claimed to have discovered it. Whatever the history of the Charge, it is a beautiful expression of the faith and practice of Wicca.

The Charge of the Goddess

Listen to the words of the Great Mother, who of old was also called Artemis, Astarte, Athena, Diana, Melusine, Aphrodite, Cerridwen, Dana, Arianrhod, Isis, Brid, and many other names:

"Whenever ye have need of any thing, once in the month, and better it be when the Moon is full, then shall ye assemble in some secret place and adore the spirit of Me Who am Queen of all Witches. There shall ye assemble, ye who are fain to learn all sorcery, yet have not won its deepest secrets; to these I will teach things that are yet unknown.

And ye shall be free from slavery, and as a sign that ye be really free, ye shall be naked in your rites; and ye shall dance, sing, feast, make music and love, all in My praise. For Mine is the ecstasy of the spirit and Mine also is joy on earth. For My Law is Love unto all beings. Keep pure your highest ideal; strive ever towards it; let naught stop you or turn you aside. For Mine is the secret door that opens upon the land of youth, and Mine is the cup of the wine of Life, and the cauldron of Cerridwen that is the holy grail of immortality. I am the gracious Goddess, who gives the gift of joy unto all hearts.

Upon Earth, I give the knowledge of the spirit eternal; and beyond death I give peace and freedom and reunion with those who have gone before. Nor do I demand aught of sacrifice, for behold, I am the Mother of all things and My Love is poured out upon the earth."

Hear ye the words of the Star Goddess, she in the dust of Whose Feet are the Hosts of Heaven, and whose body encircles the Universe:

"I Who am the beauty of the green Earth and the white Moon among the stars and the Mysteries of the waters, and the desire of all hearts, call unto thy soul. Arise and come unto Me. For I am the soul of nature who gives life to the Universe. From Me all things proceed, and unto Me all things must return; and before my face, beloved of Gods and of men, let thine innermost divine self be enfolded in the rapture of the infinite.

Let My worship be within the heart that rejoices, for behold, all acts of Love and pleasure are My rituals. And therefore let there be beauty and strength, power and compassion, honor and humility, mirth and reverence within you.

And thou who thinkest to seek for Me, know thy seeking and yearning shall avail thee not, unless thou knowest the Mystery: for if that which thou seekest, thou findest not within, then thou shall never find it without. For behold, I have been with thee from the beginning, and I am that which is attained at the end of desire."

How each group or Tradition celebrates the Sabbats and Esbats is a matter of the consensus and interest of its members. In general, Wiccans seem to be celebrating the Sabbats more regularly than the Esbats.

Rites of Passage

In creating a religion, Wiccans have addressed the various "Rites of Passage" experienced by all people throughout their lives. This is an area where Wicca is still evolving, and practices vary widely from group to group and Tradition to Tradition.

WICCANINGS (NAMINGS)

"Wiccaning" or "Naming" is the term used to describe the celebration which accompanies the birth of a child. As Wicca is nominally a fertility religion, the birth of a child is seen as a gift from the Gods and a sacred rite in itself. Once the child is born, and the life of the family has settled down a bit, the parents and community celebrate the Wiccaning of the child, the act of introducing the child to the Gods and to the Community, and asking the Goddess, God, and Community for their protection of the child as s/he grows. It is not a sealing of the child into Wicca. Wicca is a religion of choice, and where children may be placed under the protection of the Gods, the child is allowed to choose her or his religious path when old enough to make that decision. Wiccanings can take place immediately after birth or up to a year or more later. There is no set time frame.

COMING OF AGE

Celebrations of Puberty are also Wiccan rites of passage. Especially in the Feminist groups, when a girl has her first menstrual period, she is considered a woman. Many groups have the women gather for a party or celebration to honor the girl and also let her know the responsibilities of sexual maturity. Wiccans are very much choice–oriented. This includes the choice to not be sexually active, the choice not to have an abortion, to responsibly use contraceptives, and to understand the implications of being a sexual person. Just because Wicca is a fertility religion, it does not mean Wiccans engage in free sex. Quite the opposite. Personal responsibility and informed choice extends into the area of sexual activity just as much as any other area of life.

With boys, the timing of celebrating sexual maturity is less defined. It can be at the time of a boy's first wet dream, of the appearance of secondary sexual characteristics like beard and pubic hair, of his conscious assuming the "responsibilities of a man." The tradition of celebrating a boy's sexual maturity is less universal and not as formalized. The Gay men's movement currently seems to be doing the most with writing and holding rituals and celebrations in this area. Generally in them, the boy will learn about sexual responsibility, as well as celebrate his new manhood.

Wiccans view sexuality as a normal, natural part of human life. How that sexuality manifests, be it homosexual, heterosexual, bi-sexual or celibate is a private matter as long as an individual practices their sexuality within the ideals of the Wiccan Rede, *"An ye harm none, do as ye will."* Pederasty and child pornography are not tolerated at all, anywhere within Wicca.

To Wiccans the family is sacred, but Wiccans are inclusive about what they view as family. A family can be a nuclear family of parents and children, but a family might extend to grandparents, aunts, uncles and cousins. And it can include coven siblings, friends, High Priest and/or High Priestess, and co-religionists. "We are a family" is a phrase which Wiccans have readily adopted. And many Wiccans behave as if all other Wiccans are family; you may not love them, you may not get along with them, but you will come to their aid and defense if necessary.

Rites of passage help define Wiccan families and the greater Wiccan Community, which are much bigger and more diverse than most non-Wiccans would ever imagine.

THE INITIATION

Initiation is also seen as an important rite of passage. Ideally, an Initiation not only marks a stage of learning and/or achievement, it also acknowledges, or triggers, a change within. There is a definite mystical element to a good Initiation, and a person's Initiation has "taken" when they show evidence in their life of some deep inner revelation and/or change. Initiation rituals may differ little from Tradition to Tradition, but the words and ceremony are only the surface of an Initiation. The personal experience is what is important, and this cannot be understood through reading, but must be lived through and assimilated.

As Wiccaning does not guarantee a person will become Wiccan, the *choice* to take training and get an Initiation is an important rite of passage. The first step is Dedication. This is the commitment a person makes to himself or herself, to the Wiccan community, and to the Goddess and God, to learn about Wicca and study the religion and Craft. Being a Dedicant shows a certain level of commitment, yet does not confirm the full membership that Initiation does. Each Tradition and group has its own rules, but a somewhat recognized standard in Wicca is that at least a year-and-a-day must pass to progress from Dedicant to Initiate. Since Wiccan training covers the religion and practice of Wicca, including possibly the practice of magick, ethics, and divination, a year and a day may sometimes seem short. But many Dedicants may have already studied on their own, and have a head start. An important part of Initiation is learning a group's technical language, the "buzzwords," so the person can communicate effectively with others of the Tradition.

There is no specified age at which Initiation becomes an option, though many groups will not allow minors into their groups, for considerations of alcohol use and also legal protection. A fifteen-year-old may be fully informed and mature enough to make a choice of religious path, but the parents may not allow the person to actively pursue that interest. All these restrictions can result in cutting most young people off from the possibility of Wiccan training, but until society takes a more benign view of Wicca, the restrictions will probably continue to exist.

As a person learns and progresses within Wicca, there are three Initiations or Degrees available. A somewhat common phrase states, "A First Degree is responsible for themselves, a Second Degree is responsible for others of their immediate coven or group, and a Third Degree is responsible for the community as a whole." Each group and Tradition has its own definitions and levels of learning and expertise for each level. The minimum time period for progression from First to Second, and Second to Third, is again the usual "year-and-a-day."

Not all Wiccans will get all three Degrees, but ideally each Wiccan will train and study at least enough to get a First Degree. Wicca, as it is currently practiced, is a religion of "Priests," that is, each Initiate is considered to be a Priestess or Priest in his or her own right and fully capable of communicating with their Gods directly.

Some Wiccan Traditions reserve the title "High Priestess" or "High Priest" for people who have been initiated to the Third Degree. Some use that title for the leaders of a coven.

HANDFASTINGS (MARRIAGES)

Handfasting is the life passage which comes when a Wiccan wishes to be bonded to a partner in the eyes of the Gods. This may or may not also be a legal marriage. Wiccans are more broad in how they view committed partnerships. Same-sex partnerships may be celebrated just as heterosexual ones are. And a few Wiccans participate in multiple partnerships, though this is much less common. A handfasting can be for a defined period, usually not shorter than a year-and-a-day. Or a handfasting can be "until death do we part." It is up to the participants. Handfastings are celebrated much the same way as weddings, with all the variations and styles seen in modern weddings. Wiccans usually hold the rite in a Circle of some sort. The couple shares their vows, and then their hands may be bound together as a symbol of their partnership. They then may "jump the broom" together, symbolizing the household they will share. Otherwise there are few set rules. Of course, some sort of party and feast follows.

HANDPARTINGS (DIVORCE)

Handparting is the ceremony Wiccans use to mark the life passage of divorce (or the ending of a committed relationship). As handfasting is a magickal rite, so should be the ceremony of ending a relationship, which was solemnized before the Gods and Community. Oftentimes, it is not possible to get both partners together for a handparting ceremony. But when possible, the ceremony can bring closure, a concrete ending to a marriage or committed partnership. A handparting is done in a Circle, and the hands which were bound, are unbound. It can also serve to sever the emotional and magickal ties between partners, so each can go on with a life free of the other's influence. This does not mean the relationship is denied, ignored or forgotten. Just that each person is free to go his or her own way. Sometimes there is a party and feast, sometimes not. It is usually most desirable to have the person who officiated at the handfasting officiate at the handparting also.

ELDERINGS

Eldering is a relatively new tradition and rite of passage in Wicca. Modern western society has relegated older people to positions of obscurity. Wicca is openly and consciously honoring and valuing those who have lived and learned and are now valuable resources for the greater Wiccan Community. Perhaps because Wicca is for the most part a chosen religion, there are currently few Elders who have gone before and had the same experiences the younger Wiccans have. Those who do exist and who have been in the Craft for 20 years or more, are being valued. They become the wise counselors to the active leadership. They tell the stories of the times before and what it was like for them when they were young. They share their knowledge and insight. They are honored for their achievements and accomplishments.

A ceremony of Eldering is sometimes done for those who have been around for a long time and who have gravitated to the role of Elder. Sometimes the Eldering ceremony happens at menopause for women, and a similar age for men. Retirement used to be a good societal marker, but with the changing society, few can actually count on a full retirement at a set age anymore. An Eldering ceremony is similar to a Wiccaning, a party celebrating the individual and the individual's place in the family and community of Wicca. Eldering is also seen as an Initiation of sorts, though not a Degreed Initiation. Eldering can mark the time when a person gives up active leadership and gains a seat around the council fires.

PASSING OVER

Death is the last life passage each of us will experience. Wiccans view death as a natural part of life. Often some sort of reincarnation is a part of each individual's beliefs. Many Wiccans choose to start working on the death passage before actual death. If a person is known to be dying, Wiccans will often make an effort to visit the person, talk and make their peace with him or her, or at least visit one last time. Hopefully, the person who is dying will not be fearful or anxious about the coming final Initiation. Wiccans will be sad at the coming loss, but also hopeful of a rest in the Summerlands, a place where Wiccans go between lives. It is said to be a place of eternal summer, warm, green, and pleasant. The spirits of those who have gone before are there and will greet the person upon arrival. Those who have passed away are still among us in spirit, and they can manifest themselves to the living in various ways. Many Wiccans have had what they consider to be concrete proof that there is a life after death. The dying person will try to make peace with the world, and prepare for the transition ahead. In any case, the Wiccan death passage hopefully starts before the actual death, so the person who is dying can take part and express his or her wishes.

BURIAL OF THE DEAD

The Wiccan memorial celebration is not as codified as the other life passages are. Death is a natural part of life. Wiccans celebrate the mystery of death each year at Samhain, so we already have a yearly mourning period set aside in one of our eight Sabbats. A Wiccan memorial can consist of a Circle and a group singing of the "Lyke Wake Dirge" which although a song, is a magical Circle and rite in and of itself, and celebrates the cyclic nature of life and death. Some groups will have a Circle in which each person offers a short memorial about the deceased. There may be prayers for an easy passage or a pleasant sojourn in the Summerlands. In the case of a sudden death, there may have been psychic trauma for the soul of the deceased (which is one theory for the existence of "ghosts"). Then the person may need help to spiritually pass beyond. The group will try to aid in this with prayer and loving energy which can help the spirit on its journey to the Summerlands.

Modern Wicca has had relatively few older people, so natural death isn't a thing which has become routine. On the other hand, death through AIDS and other diseases, or by accident are very common. Because Wicca is a less mainstream religion, often the Wiccan "Crossing Over," or funeral ceremony is held without the deceased or the family or most friends present. It is rare that a Wiccan can be openly mourned and buried as Wiccan. Usually the Wiccan ceremony is held after the "mundane" services and burial, often in the Covenstead. For this reason, Wiccans seem ambivalent about memorials and burial rites. Often they have little or no say in these, the wishes of their surviving, often non-Wiccan, families being paramount. The secrecy of being Wiccan often extends even into one's birth family.

Wiccans have little preferences in regard to body disposal. Some prefer cremation (it's more ecologically sound), some want burial, and some express no preference, knowing their families will do what they will. The idea of special reverence for the dead body is illogical to most Wiccans, as the true self is the soul or spirit, and body is merely the fleshly vehicle. Once dead, the essence lives on, and the body is no longer needed. No matter what time of year a Wiccan dies, s/he will be remembered at the next Samhain, for that is what Samhain is for, remembrance of those who have passed on before.

Working the Sacred

SACRED SPACE AND CIRCLE STRUCTURE

Sacred Space is a term Wiccans use to define the area within a Magickal Circle which has been defined, Cleansed, and Consecrated for ritual use, be it for a celebration or a Working. Within a Magickal Circle, Holy Ground is created, even if only for a short time. Sacred Space is deemed as holy as a Christian altar or the Ark in a Temple. However, Sacred Space is usually temporary, as Wiccans have few permanent church buildings. Wiccans also believe that the Goddess and God are everywhere, so there is no urgent need for special buildings set apart from the rest of the world. Many Wiccans prefer to worship in nature when weather permits. Some groups meet in private homes or rented space for the Sabbats.

The Magickal Circle is created anew each time. There is no one set formula for how a circle should go, but there are some guidelines of what elements need to be present for a circle to be a circle. Different Traditions may mandate different circles for different occasions. However, these are some basic steps for creating, using, and taking down the Magickal Circle.

1. *Scribing the Circle* means outlining the area to be Cleansed and Consecrated and defining the boundaries the Energy will be contained within.

2. *Cleansing the Circle* involves making the circle free of stray or unwanted Energies and/or beings—making a clean slate to work upon, so to speak.

3. *Calling the Quarters* (or Watchtowers) invites guardian entities in to watch over and protect the circle, entities that

are allied to the participants (e.g., the Gods) to aid in the Working.

4. *The Binding* is the act of declaring that the circle is cast and ready for whatever the Wiccan is doing.

5. *Calling in the Goddess and God* may entail Evoking the Goddess and God into the circle, that is, inviting them to come and watch as guests or observers. Or it may entail Invoking them into the Priestess and Priest presiding over the circle, which means bringing them into the Working as principals along with the Priestess and Priest. When Invoking, the Priestess and Priest do not give up their bodies to the Gods, but rather share their bodies with the Gods and act in partnership. This is usually done only within a properly Consecrated Circle, under controlled conditions, and only for a specific length of time. When Calling In the Goddess and God, there are usually candles, sometimes one black and one white symbolizing the Goddess and God and their presence within the circle and everywhere.

6. *The Working* can range from a celebration of a Sabbat or Esbat, to a full magickal ritual to effect change in an individual or the world. Generally it is commonly considered proper to put up a circle only for a specific purpose. Some Traditions mandate that there must be some sort of magick performed within a circle each time one is erected. Some Traditions consider celebration or teaching to be purpose enough for a circle.

Once the Working is finished and the energy of it is properly grounded, the Wiccan takes down the circle in reverse order of how it was erected.

7. *Dismissing the Gods* closes the Evoking or Invoking with thanks and love and allows the Goddess and God to return to their realms.

8. *Dismissing the Quarters or Watchtowers* sends them back to their ethereal realms.

9. *Taking Up the Circle* is where all the remaining energy that was Invoked or used during the Working is returned to where it came from.

10. *Opening the Circle* means you are done when you declare the circle is open.

Ideally, there should be no evidence of a circle left in the area. If outdoors, Wiccans are very careful to clean up anything they've brought and whatever others brought earlier which does not belong in the area. Most parks and campgrounds are very happy to host Wiccan and Pagan events, as the area usually ends up cleaner at the end than when the event started. This is one way Wiccans manifest their belief that all nature is sacred. Indoors at a temporary site, Wiccans sweep and clean up. In a home there may be more-or-less permanent altar furnishings which are left up, but the candles and other physical trappings, as well as whatever energies were raised in the circle, are cleaned up so the room returns to normal.

When a circle is up, Wiccans are very careful to not cross the circle boundary without acknowledgment and precautions. This is because a circle is Sacred Space and to violate it carelessly shows a lack of respect, and can also disrupt the energies and spoil the Working. The circle may be intangible to the naked eye, but for someone who is sensitive to such things, it is very real. Most dogs will not cross a circle boundary. And although most cats will show by their behavior that they are aware a circle is up, being cats, they will generally move in and out of a circle at their whim. Small children, too, may move in and out of a properly constructed circle without harm, but they can be distracting. Whether or not children are to be involved is best determined beforehand. It's good to remember that little children and cats are generally much more sensitive to the psychic/spiritual world than most adults, so they may be used as a rough gauge of how things are going. If, for instance, your previously content sleeping pussycat takes off at a dead run for parts unknown, or every baby within earshot starts screaming, you just might just want to check on what's going on.

When a circle is violated, either by accident or on purpose, the ritual is disrupted, and additional cleansing may be needed. Some groups might actually start over, while other groups might just close down the circle and abandon the attempt. When Wiccans are disturbed during a ritual held outdoors, either by passersby or occasionally by police or other summoned officials, they can get quite upset if those who come in are not understanding or respectful of the Sacred Space which is created. This is not to say that Wiccans expect just anyone to be aware of a circle, but they do hope that after an explanation the intruders will be respectful and moderate in their actions, giving the people time to close down the circle before barging in with intrusions. Wiccans see the disruption of a circle in the same way a Christian might view disrespectful intrusion on a church service or invasion of Hallowed Ground. Because many law enforcement departments are not aware of the religious implications of the disruption of a Wiccan Circle, they can cause animosity. Many Wiccan groups will not hold circles outdoors without assurances they will not be disturbed (usually getting the appropriate permits is enough). Some municipalities are much more Wiccan friendly than others. Some Wiccan groups have engaged in educational activities for their local law enforcement communities, so such misunderstandings will not take place. Unfortunately there is still much misunderstanding of Wiccans and prejudice against them, even though there is the Constitutional right to freedom of religion in the U.S. Wiccans are becoming more active and aggressive in asserting their right to be treated as any other religious group.

PENTAGRAMS

Two separate pentagrams are used in Wiccan Circles. These are the Invoking pentagram and the Banishing pentagram. The Invoking pentagram is drawn with a clockwise, deosil, or sunwise motion. The Banishing Pentagram is drawn with a counterclockwise, widdershins, or moonwise motion. Which point you start the pentagram at is a topic of contention among several Traditions. There are books which illustrate numerous pentagrams both from Wicca and High Magick, describing which point symbolizes which element and many other details. For this circle we don't need to go into all of that. Illustrated here are the Invoking and Banishing Pentagrams used by Estelle and Paul. They are more simplistic and generic than most, but they work. The Invoking pentagram is used when calling in the Elements (or Watchtowers or Quarters, whatever you might want to call them), and the Banishing Pentagram is used when dismissing them.

Figure #1 – Pentagrams

Elemental Pentagram

Invoking Pentagram   ## Banishing Pentagram

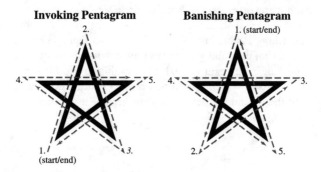

ELEMENTAL CROSS

The Elemental Cross is an equal-armed cross. There is also a three-dimensional form which is six-armed: up, down, left, right, in, and out. This is a variation of an ancient symbol known as the "Sun Wheel," and it can function like a pentagram. In this circle, it is used for Cleansing. If you want to create a circle but not use a pentagram, the elemental cross is an acceptable and effective substitute. You might not want to use a pentagram, because a pentagram can create a strong resonating signal on the astral plane. It calls attention to you for anything or anyone who cares to come and investigate. There are times when a person might not want to attract attention on that level, and those times are when an elemental cross is desirable.

Following is a diagram of the elemental cross. To aid in remembering which direction goes with which arm, Estelle visualizes a map of the United States, and then does the cross for each quarter over the map. It's simple but effective. When doing the elemental cross, start with the arm of the direction (East for East, South for South and so on), and then go around clockwise. For the three-dimensional cross, start with the Quarter you are facing, go clockwise, and end with an "in" and an "out" for the third dimension.

Figure #2 – The Elemental Cross

Elemental Cross

Earth
North

Water
West

Air
East

Spirit
Center

Fire
South

Elemental Cross in Two Dimentions

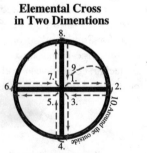

11. Go Back & Front
12. Around the Middle

Elemental Cross in Three Dimentions

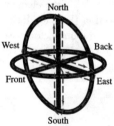

North

West

Back

Front

East

South

SACRED TOOLS

Wicca has occasionally been described as "a religion of stuff," with a tremendous variety of tools and other items used in a myriad of ways. Some of the most common sacred tools are the Athame, the Cup, the Pentacle, and the Wand.

The Athame

The first and most visibly obvious Wiccan Ritual Tool is the Athame—the sacred knife used to "divide this from that" and direct Magickal Energies. The kind of knife used varies from Tradition to Tradition and from individual to individual. It is suggested in Craft lore that an Athame is a black-handled, double-edged knife with a six inch blade, about ten to twelve inches in total length. Most prefer a knife with a handle of some natural material, be it wood, leather, or bone. Knives can also come with handles of rubber, micarta, or metal, but these are considered by some to be less desirable as these materials are less natural. They all have been refined, processed, or altered substantially in some way from their original state. Plastic is also used as a knife handle material, and it is considered totally artificial. Personal preference can vary widely. Generally you get the best that's available within the constraints of your budget. You can always "trade up" later.

To Wiccans this knife is a Sacred Tool and would never be used as a weapon. It is also very personal. For one to touch another's Athame without permission is considered a gross violation of personal space. The Athame is used to direct Magickal Energies and to cast the circle, drawing out and defining the area that is to make up the circle. It is also used when Calling and Dismissing the Quarters and doing other types of Workings. To an outsider it might look as if a Wiccan in a circle is just waving a knife around, but the use of the Athame is specific and controlled. The Athame symbolizes the element of either fire or air depending on the Tradition.

An issue of contention between Wiccans and law enforcement is the use of the Athame. Police generally only see the knives, and often react to what they justifiably perceive to be a threat. Wiccans, on the other hand, see their Athames as Sacred Tools and can be offended if asked to put them away or angered if asked to hand them over. Education on both sides, before problems develop, is the best way to avoid these conflicts. If you travel to rituals and want to bring your Athame, it should be sheathed and placed in some bag or case, so it is not visible nor readily at hand. Keeping it suitably stored in your car trunk while in transit is a good idea. Remember, most states and cities have blade laws, and the average "legal knife," is single-edged with a blade of no more than three inches in length. Check your local state and city ordinances for the specifics where you live. Your Athame is a Sacred Tool to you, but most law enforcement personnel will not view it as such, and will err on the side of caution—their caution.

Wiccans usually choose to avoid public areas to avoid having to deal with possible misunderstandings. As Wicca becomes more widely recognized and better understood, these clashes will hopefully become less and less frequent.

The simplest substitute for an actual metal Athame is the first two fingers of the right hand, raised and used to direct the Energies as if you were pointing with two fingers. This "Athame" has the advantage of not being threatening nor easily confiscated, and is legal everywhere you want to go. It may take a bit of practice, but it can be just as effective as a metal Athame when used correctly.

The Cup

The Cup is used to hold wine (or a non-alcoholic substitute), and it symbolizes the womb, among other things. The act of blessing the wine symbolizes the procreative act and is called the Great Rite. Wicca celebrates nature and fertility and this is the most visible manifestation of that. Most Traditions feel that the Cup symbolizes the element of water. Our blessing of the wine and ritual cakes is similar to Christian Communion.

The Pentacle

The Pentacle is generally considered a symbol of the element of earth. It is usually a disk or plate with a pentagram (five-pointed star) on it. Traditionally, the pentacle was made of wax so it could be easily destroyed in emergencies. Nowadays, with the "burning times" over, pentacles can be made of wood, metal, stone, or other more permanent materials. The pentacle rests on the Altar and is used for Grounding the Energies of a ritual, as well as possibly holding the cakes and wine before they are blessed and shared.

The Wand

The Wand is most simply a stick, usually about 18 inches in length, and it is used to direct Magickal Energies, though in a different way than the Athame. Some Traditions use Wands to hold energies or spells, others use them in Casting the Circle. Wands can be just plain wooden sticks, or very elaborate creations of various materials with crystals and designs and the rest. The Wand can most commonly be used to symbolize either the element of air or fire (whichever one of these two elements is *not* represented by the Athame), depending upon the Tradition.

Other Tools

While the Athame, Cup, Pentacle, and Wand are the four main Sacred Tools of Wicca, there are many other items used by various people in various ritual ways. Some of the other common tools are:

- the Sword, sort of an overgrown Athame;
- the Staff, like a big Wand, but also with other uses;
- an incense holder and incense;
- candles and candle holders;
- a bowl for water and a holder for salt, both used in Cleansing;
- statues or pictures of the Goddess and God;
- sacred garb or ritual clothing;
- Cords or braided belts, used as symbols of degree recognition as well as measuring devices for scribing the circle;
- the Altar itself, which can be as simple as a cloth on the ground, more substantial, like a card table, or permanent, made of wood or stone;
- the Broom or Besom, used by Wiccans today more for cleansing and not for flying. In cleansing, an area is swept clean of unwanted energies as well as dirt. (The broom is also used in Handfastings or weddings, during which the newly joined couple "Jumps the Broom," symbolizing their setting up housekeeping together).

Wiccans have a penchant for collecting tools and ritual items. Craft lore states that you must never bargain when buying a ritual item. In other words, you don't haggle over the price. Some people, however, like getting goodies at garage sales and feel that bargaining is a sacred act in itself. How someone views this matter is individual or a matter of Traditional belief.

Craft tools should always be Cleansed and Consecrated before use. They are considered Sacred objects and it is impolite and disrespectful to touch or use another person's tools without their permission. Some tools are highly personal (most prominently the Athame), while other tools are for general use, like candles or incense. A good rule to use when attending a Wiccan function: "Don't touch anyone's anything without permission, ever."

Casting a
Basic Wiccan Circle

Described below is a basic Wiccan Circle, which can be modified to suit individual purposes. Most circles are similar, and the circle outlined in the following pages has all the requisite elements of a good solid circle. We encourage you to look further and see what other circles are out there—there are endless possible variations. Some groups use the same circle every time, while other Traditions mandate a different circle be cast for each specific type of Working. Other groups use a slightly different circle each time. What's important is that all the basic elements be present, so that the Energies are built and contained properly.

The act of creating a circle is known as "casting a circle." A circle, when fully formed, is a thing which is solid and tangible to those who are able to sense it. However, it is meant to be transitory. It is cast or put up or created for a specific time, and when that time is up, it is then taken down, banished, or sent away. Some groups use "circle" as a verb, as in "Will you be circling with us tonight?" (meaning "Will you join us in our circle?" or "Will you help us create a circle?"). The act of casting a circle is a process with specific steps and rules, which creates a thing that is then later destroyed. Perhaps "used up" is a better phrase. Casting a circle can be likened to preparing a meal. You have to buy the food, get out the utensils, prepare and cook the food, and set the table. This is analogous to the casting of the circle. When the cooking and other preparations are finished, the meal is served and you eat. This is analogous to the Working. After the meal is finished and the food has been consumed, you have to clean the utensils used, wash the dishes, and tidy up. This is analogous to banishing the circle.

There are endless debates among the various Traditions about Altar placement and the Quarter you begin from. North and East are the most commonly favored directions. In actuality, the energies will usually work no matter where your Altar is placed or which Quarter you start in. All that really matters is that you are consistent within each circle, and you concentrate and correctly visualize the energies as you build it.

This circle can be cast with a High Priestess (HPS), a High Priest (HP), and a group, with just an HPS and an HP, or with one individual taking both parts. The circle can be done all male or all female with one person doing both parts, or better, two people, each one taking a part. In the latter case the terms HPS and HP refer to the "receptive" and "active" principles respectively. The roles are not necessarily gender specific. You can also call on just the Goddess (as Dianic groups do) or just the God, but the energies may not be as balanced as they are when calling on both.

RITUAL TOOLS

The circle uses fairly standard ritual tools. The items and equipment listed here are pretty basic, and maybe 90% of all Wiccans use similar tools in their circles. There are many others that can be used, with specific properties and meanings. Substitutions can be made (such as pictures or objects for the Quarters). There is no "one right, true, and only way" to build a circle, nor even *the* set of required ritual implements or equipment. Just use whatever works best for you and is available.

There are items and actions that are optional and are marked as such. The circle will still be up and effective without them, but some people like the little extra touches the options provide. It's a matter of preference. The Altar itself can be a permanent stone altar, a wooden altar, or a portable altar (like a card table), or maybe just a cloth on the ground. Whatever adapts itself to the place you are in and the materials and resources available is fine.

Immediately following you will find a description of casting a fairly standard Wiccan Circle. Magickal Directions are <u>underlined</u>. Stage Directions are {indented and enclosed in braces}. "Speeches are *in bold italics and enclosed in quotation marks.*" Note—for simplicity, brevity, and ease of reading the text uses HPS (High Priestess) with she and her and HP (High Priest) with he and his. This is because standard Wiccan convention has a female HPS and a male HP. However, any person may take the part of the HPS and/or HP, and as long as they realize that the HPS is the receptive principle and the HP is the active principle, the energies will work.

A Circle Ritual
(Step 1) <u>Assemble the following items for the Altar:</u>
- reading candle and holder
- "Presence" candles (2)
- lighter or matches
- candle snuffer (optional, but an elegant touch)
- Athame
- chalice and libation (typically wine, cider, some other juice, or water)
- plate of cakes
- Pentacle

- incense holder with your favorite incense
- salt holder and salt
- water holder and water
- Wand
- bell and striker (optional)
- Quarter candles and candle holders (4); (1 for each Quarter) (optional)

(Step 2) <u>Pre-ritual preparations:</u>
{Perform whatever personal "cleansing" you feel is needed to be done by yourself and the other participants. Dress in a manner that makes you feel "special" and "magickal," for example, special robes or jewelry.

Assemble your Altar, and set up your Quarter candles (please refer to the diagram below).

Close the drapes, unplug the phone, lock the door (all to reduce possible interruptions).}

Figure #3 – Altar Set-Up

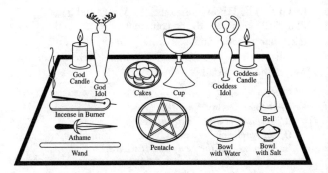

(Step 3) <u>Begin the Circle</u>:
{Light your (a) reading, (b) Quarter, and (c) Presence candles.}

    Optional—{The HP goes to the altar and rings the bell three times to Cleanse the area and to focus the attention of the participants, preparatory to "Scribing" the circle.}

(Step 4) <u>The HP Scribes the Circle</u>:
{Using his Athame, the HP "Scribes," or draws a circle in the air around the assembled gathering, beginning either at the East or the North Quarter. Whichever point you choose, start in that same Quarter for everything that is done in the circle, and move deosil.}

Note: Most Traditions feel that all movement within a circle by all participants should be in a deosil or clockwise direction. This is so the Energies are not accidentally banished by moving widdershins or counterclockwise. If you need to turn to the left, make a three-quarter (or whatever) deosil turn around to where you need to face. It will feel strange at first, but eventually it will be natural to move only deosil in a circle. This is important.

(Step 5) <u>The HPS Consecrates the Water and Salt</u>:
{The HPS first goes to the container of water on the Altar, takes her Athame and places its point in the water, then visualizes all negative Energies being driven out of the water. She says aloud:}

> *"I Exorcise thee, O creature of Water,*
> *That thou cast out from thee*
> *All Impurities and Uncleanliness*
> *Of the spirits of Phantasm*
> *In the names of the Lady and the Lord."*

{Here and throughout, you may substitute the names of any particular Goddess and/or God you choose.

The HPS then takes the tip of her Athame and, putting it into the salt, visualizes all negative Energies being driven out of the salt, and says:}

"Blessings upon thee, O creature of Earth.
Let all malignancies and hindrances
Pass forth and let all goodness enter in."

{The HPS then takes three tips of salt on her Athame and puts them in the water. She says:}

"As we are ever mindful
That as water purifies the body,
So salt purifies the soul."

{The HPS then stirs the salt into the water. When finished she wipes her blade dry. She says:}

"Wherefore I do bless thee
In the names of the Lady and the Lord,
That thou mayest aid me."

(Step 6) <u>The HPS then Aspurges, or Cleanses, the Circle with Earth and Water:</u>

{Taking the water container, and starting in the Quarter of choice, moving deosil, the HPS sprinkles the consecrated water three times at each Quarter, also Above and Below. The Altar may also be sprinkled, to cleanse it, as well. This sprinkling should be light, a couple of drops on the end of the fingers.}

(Step 7) <u>The HP then Consecrates the Fire and Air</u>:
{The HP takes the incense and lights it in one of the candles. He says:}

>*"I charge thee, O Creature of Fire,*
>*That thou allow no evil to defile this Circle."*

{The HP then extinguishes the flame and watching the incense curl up, he says:}

>*"I invoke thee, O creature of Air,*
>*That thou may protect this our Circle with love."*

(Step 8) <u>The HP then Censes, or Cleanses, the Circle with</u>
<u>Fire and Air</u>:
{Beginning in the chosen Quarter, the HP then censes the circle using the burning incense by drawing, in the air, the appropriate Elemental Cross in each Quarter, then, moving deosil, finishes in the center of the circle using a full 3-D Elemental Cross.}

Figure #4 – The 3-D Elemental Cross

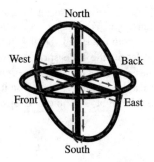

(Step 9) <u>The HPS then Invokes the Quarter Guardians</u>:
{The HPS now takes her Athame, and starting at the Quarter of choice, draws an Invoking Pentagram in each Quarter, moving deosil around the circle.}

Figure #5 – An Invoking Pentagram

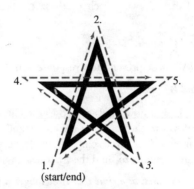

{After each pentagram has been drawn, she says:}

"Guardians of the Watchtowers of the _____,
Creatures of _____, {East/Air, South/Fire, West/Water,
North/Earth}
I welcome thee and ask that you witness this rite
and guard this Circle and all within.
Hail and Welcome!" {East/Air, South/Fire, West/Water,
North/Earth}

{All those present now respond with:}

"Hail and Welcome!"

Note: *You should fill in the appropriate direction and element of each of the above Quarters, starting with the Quarter of choice.*

{The HPS finally moves to the center of the circle, makes an Invoking Pentagram while pointing first Above and then Below.}

Optional: {After drawing each of these pentagrams, the HPS says:}

> *"Hail and Welcome."*

Optional: {All those present now response with:}

> *"Hail and Welcome!"*

(Step 10) <u>The HP now Binds or Closes the Circle:</u>
{The HP moves to the center of the circle, and taking the Wand he moves deosil, retracing the circle he previously drew with his Athame, to Bind the Energies, saying:}

> *"Thus we are met, at a time that is no longer a time,*
> *in a place that is no longer a place,*
> *for we are between the worlds and beyond.*
> *May the Goddess and God*
> *help and protect us on our Magickal journey.*
> *So Mote It Be!"*

{All those present now respond with:}

> *"So Mote It Be!"*

(Step 11) <u>The Goddess and God are called:</u>
{The HPS and HP stand together at the Altar facing each other, holding hands: one hand up, one down.}

{If your circle is to be an Evocation—inviting the Goddess and God to the party—you might say:}

> **"Lady and Lord,**
> **we ask for your presence at this, our Circle.**
> **May you guard and watch over our Circle,**
> **and guide us with your loving presences.**
> **So Mote It Be!"**

{All those present now respond with:}

> **"So Mote It Be!"**

{If the circle is to be an "Invocation"—inviting the presences of the Goddess and God into the High Priestess and High Priest—you might say:}

> **"Lady and Lord,**
> **we invite you to be present within our Circle.**
> **Be present within our High Priestess and High Priest**
> **that you might participate fully in our rites.**
> **Share their bodies and senses**
> **and open their hearts to your Love.**
> **Be here with us in our Circle now.**
> **So Mote It Be!"**

{All those present should respond with:}

> **"So Mote It Be!"**

(Step 12) <u>Insert "Working" here</u>:
{Here is the heart of the ritual, be it a celebration or magickal working or both. The Working can be a celebration of a Sabbat or Esbat, it can be an Initiation, or a cleansing, consecration, banishing, healing or divination, it can be a spell designed to change yourself or the world around you. It can also be a combination of several of these elements.

Within the bounds of the magickal circle you have a safe space to raise energy and perform magick. This is the part which takes the most time and utilizes the energy which has been contained and brought forth. Once the energy has been raised and used, then sent on its way to accomplish what you want at the end of your Working, the rest of the ritual is to "Seal" the working, banish any excess energies, and take down the circle.}

(Step 13) <u>Perform The Great Rite</u>:
{The Great Rite is the Wiccan form of Communion. To perform it, the High Priestess holds the Cup in front of the High Priest, who is holding his Athame, blade down, over the Cup. First the HPS says:}

> *"As the Cup is the Female;"*

{Then the HP:}

> *"And the Athame is the Male;"*

{As they each say their words, they are slowly bringing the Cup and Athame together, so the blade of the Athame is dipped into the libation. The High Priestess and High Priest should feel the Power of the Goddess and God enter the libation. And they both say:}

> *"Together they are One!"*

{After the blade is removed it is wiped clean. The High Priestess raises the cup in salute to the Gods and drinks. She then hands the cup to the High Priest saying:}

> *"Blessed Be."*

{The High Priest then raises the cup in salute and also drinks, saying:}

"Blessed Be."

{Then the HPS takes the plate of cakes, and the HP holds his hands over them, and they bless them, both saying:)

"Lady and Lord,
bless these cakes
that we may partake of your bounty."

{The HPS takes a cake and eats it, and the HP does the same. The Cup and cakes are then passed around the circle so that all may share.

Once the Cup has passed all around the circle, it is handed back to the HPS who then drinks any remaining libation (If there is too much for her to drink alone, she may pass it to others who help drain the liquid to a manageable level.) The HPS drains the Cup, places it upside down on the pentacle (along with the last few drops of libation, for the Gods), and Grounds the Energy of the ritual through the pentacle. If there are cakes left they are also placed on the Altar.}

Note: You can pass the Cup and cakes around the circle either male to female and vice versa or just person to person. If it is male to female and there are more of one than the other, the HPS or HP interposes, to maintain the alternating pattern.

If a person has a cold or does not want to drink the libation (for instance if it is alcohol and the person does not drink alcohol) s/he can either raise the Cup in salute or dip a finger in the Cup and bring it to the lips. That is sufficient. If there is a problem with alcohol, you might substitute apple cider, non-alcoholic wine, or grape juice.

If there are too many people in the Circle for each to get a sip from the Cup, it is permissible to refill the Cup at appropriate intervals, but it should be refilled from a partially full state, not totally drained. The original container should sit beside the Altar, waiting for refill if needed. There should be enough cakes for all, or each should only take part of a cake to ensure each gets some. If a person cannot eat the cakes, s/he may just raise the plate in salute to honor the Gods.

It is considerate to announce beforehand the ingredients of the cakes and the Cup so that people can ascertain if they can or wish to partake.

(Step 14) <u>Dismiss the Goddess and God</u>:
{The HPS and HP face each other and join hands as above in Step 11.}

{If the Goddess and God were "Evoked," they say:}

> *"Lady and Lord,*
> *we thank you for joining us in our Circle.*
> *We ask for your Blessings and Love*
> *as you depart to your chosen realms.*
> *Hail and Farewell!"*

{All those present now respond with:}

> *"Hail and Farewell!"*

{If the Goddess and God were "Invoked," they say:}

> *"Lady and Lord,*
> *we thank you for your presence in our Circle.*
> *We ask for your Blessings and Love,*
> *and as you depart to your chosen realms we bid you*
> *Hail and Farewell!"*

{All those present again respond with:}

"Hail and Farewell!"

(Step 15) <u>Dismiss the Quarters</u>:
{The HPS takes her Athame and moving deosil around the circle she makes a Banishing Pentagram at each Quarter, and says:)

"Guardians of the Watchtowers of the _____,
Creatures of _____,
we thank you for your presence at this our Circle.
May there be peace between us, now and always,
and as you depart, we bid you
Hail and Farewell."

Optional—{All those present respond with:}

"Hail and Farewell."

Figure #6 – A Banishing Pentagram

(Step 16) <u>Ground and Cut the Circle</u>:

{The HP finally takes his Athame and erases the circle he drew in Step 4.

When he has done that, he then makes a cut with his Athame across where the boundary of the Circle had been, and says:}

"The Circle is open, but unbroken."

{Then at last, all those present respond with:}

"Merry meet, merry part,
and merry meet again!"

(Step 17) <u>Clean Up</u>:

{Clean up what ever food and liquid are left, and put the dishes in the sink.

Put away all the candles and disassemble your Altar.

Change back into your mundane clothes. Reconnect the phone, open the drapes and unlock the door.}

It is done.

The Characteristics
of Magick

The most basic definition of Magick is *"a controlled use of will to effect a change in one's self or surroundings."* The popular use of the term magic, without the "k," refers to stage magic, prestidigitation, and other flashy entertainments, which use misdirection and other theatrical tricks to appear to effect change through supernatural means. The "k" was added to magick to distinguish psychic–based work from stage magic. Wiccans employ magick like ceremonial magicians and other mystical/fraternal/spiritual groups, as a tool for contact with Deity and for self-development. Wiccans will use magick to effect change in themselves and the world around them, often simultaneously. Sometimes a change in the world can be made by a simple change in the basic mental outlook or perspective of an individual. In the "Magickal Realms," one can also be closer to Deity, and use Its help and guidance to make oneself a better person. One may use a specific technique such as ceremonial magick, meditation, divination, sacred song, and ecstatic dance to effect a change in mind and outlook, which takes the person out of the ordinary everyday world into the "Higher Realms." Wiccans use magick in controlled settings with controlled techniques to prevent unwanted results. Although Wiccans acknowledge no Devil, they do recognize the phenomenon of "possession" and work to avoid it.

Wiccans practice magick in circles, an area of Sacred Space which is Cleansed and secured from unwanted outside influences. This is very important, as doing magick outside of a circle is more difficult and subject to unwanted and unexpected influences and changes. The circle Wiccans put up for magick is the same as a circle for worship. Worship and magick may be combined in one Working. Some Wiccans consider magick to be a form of worship, or focused and directed prayer. Deity is always invited to participate, as Wiccans believe we are friends and co-workers with the Gods and they help us in all we do.

Wiccans practice what is termed "White Magick," magick done for the benefit of all the people involved. They do not send Energy to anyone who is not aware of it, or does not want it, as this is considered to be one type of "Black Magick," which is magick that either harms someone or imposes your Will over someone. Even healing without permission is considered a form of Black Magick because it imposes your Will. The Law of Three and the Wiccan Rede are very broad rules which apply in many more cases than are first apparent.

When a person is hurt and in need of healing Energies, and his or her direct permission cannot be obtained, most Wiccans will send the Energy "to the Cosmos," to be used however the person needs it. If they do not want to take the Energy, that is their choice, conscious or unconscious.

When practiced properly and ethically, magick is a powerful tool for effecting change in oneself and one's environment. Generally, most Wiccans do spells for themselves or for their friends or fellow Wiccans. It is easier to effect change within oneself than in the entire world around you.

GROUNDING AND CENTERING

The first magickal technique most Wiccans learn is Grounding and Centering. This gets you into a relaxed mental state, clears your mind of distractions, and focuses and contains Energy. It can be like a meditative state, but it gets you ready to act and move, as well as to sit and use your mind.

A Grounding and Centering Ritual

(Step 1) {Sit in a chair with your feet flat on the floor, your hands resting in your lap, and your spine straight.}

(Step 2) {Take three deep breaths and let them out slowly. As you let them out, relax your body, and let your tensions flow out. This is called "Taking Three Cleansing Breaths."}

(Step 3) {Once you are relaxed, imagine roots extending from your feet and the base of your spine, growing deep into the earth.}

(Step 4) {Feel yourself in your body, in your skin. Feel the gravity holding you in your chair.

As the roots grow, feel yourself rooted where you are, in the here and now, in the space you are occupying.}

(Step 5) {As you concentrate on being in the here and now, your mind should become free of extraneous thought and distractions. You should become more calm and relaxed.}

This feeling of being calm, relaxed, and firmly where you are is what Wiccans describe as being grounded and centered. The act of Grounding and Centering is the first step for any Working, be it magick or celebration. You should ground and center before starting any circle.

There are many other techniques for grounding and centering. Some are more elaborate, and some work instantaneously. Repeating to yourself a "mantra" or catch phrase is a good technique. Just using the Three Cleansing Breaths can be enough for someone who is well practiced. As you practice, it becomes easier. All the techniques involve deliberately relaxing the body, becoming mentally aware of being in the here-and-now, clearing the mind of distractions, and focusing your thoughts for whatever is to come. Grounding and centering becomes useful for many everyday life activities. If you become upset or agitated, it can help calm the emotions and get the mind clear so action can be taken. If you have a health condition, grounding and centering can sometimes help lessen physical symptoms. You can ground and center before that big meeting or job interview, and you will find your mind is more organized.

These techniques are not at all exclusive to Wicca. Many self-help disciplines use these same techniques. Most schools of meditation use some forms of grounding and centering, though they are frequently less active. If you have a technique you already use, and it works for you, then stick with it. But it is recommended you try the technique described above just to see how it might differ. There is also no psychic danger in grounding and centering. This will not psychically or spiritually "open you up" to anything. It does not make you susceptible to possession, and, in fact, centering yourself is your first defense against any type of "psychic attack." It does not put you in touch with anything. It just allows you to relax, clear your mind, and focus your thoughts. That's all. Period.

SHIELDING

Shielding is a technique in which you form a focused Energy barrier around yourself to protect yourself from outside influences.

A Shielding Ritual

(Step 1) {First Ground and Center, as described above.}

(Step 2) {Now relaxed and free of distractions, gather your internal Energy. To do this, visualize a golden sphere of light about the size of a golf ball, either in your chest area or in your forehead, depending upon which feels better to you.}

(Step 3) {Once you have that ball of light, project it outward until it floats in front of you, about two feet from your body.}

(Step 4) {Now, slowly take that Energy ball and move it around your body in a circle. Get it moving faster and faster until it becomes a golden hoop of Energy encircling your body.}

(Step 5) {Then, when you have the hoop, rotate the hoop so it turns into a sphere. This becomes a golden sphere of light which totally encircles you.}

(Step 6) {Now you anchor this golden Energy sphere with a beam of light reaching straight up to the Cosmos. You can also anchor the sphere of light with another beam of light to the eastern horizon, where the first light of the Sun appears. This connects you to the Gods and their Energies.}

This bubble you have created is elastic and personalized. It expands as you stand or move, and it contracts if you sit. This golden bubble of Energy is your Shield. It is translucent, you can see through it, but stray energies and influences cannot penetrate it. It may be invisible to you until you come up against energies from outside. And because you have created this shielding bubble of energy largely within your own mind, it should be invisible to most everyone else. The bubble can also be contracted to fit around your skin, like an outer suit of "energy wear." If you think of the "energy shields" around the space ships in television shows like *Star Trek*, you have a good idea of what Shields are and what they do.

As you become more adept at shielding, you can create bubbles of energy around your living space, your car, or other possessions. Just project the energy ball to rotate around whatever you want to Shield. Shields are not permanent. They last for a time, depending on how strongly you made the Shield and how much extraneous psychic energy is around. You have to renew your Shields every so often. The more you do these techniques, the better you get and the more quickly you can erect or reinforce a Shield. Start small with shielding yourself. Once you get comfortable with that, then try shielding your living environment. From that, you should be ready to shield other items.

Grounding, centering, and shielding are valuable techniques for living in today's hectic world. Shielding yourself while you sleep can make for a more restful night.

TOOL CLEANSINGS

The Working of Cleansing and Consecration is a ritual which most every Wiccan performs. Below is a condensed version of a simple Cleansing and Consecration ritual. As before, "Magickal Directions" are <u>Underlined</u>. "Stage Directions" are {indented and enclosed in braces}. "Speeches" are *"in bold italics and enclosed in quotation marks."*

A Tool Consecration Ritual

(Step 1) In addition to your typical set of ritual equipment, for the Magickal Working of a Cleansing, you will need:

- water and salt
- incense
- sacred oil (scented or unscented)

(Step 2) Pre-ritual Preparations:

{First, physically clean the tool by washing, polishing or whatever.

Before the Working, a person might want to inscribe the item to be Consecrated with a magickal sigil or personal Craft name or motto. This can be done permanently, as in carving into the wood handle of a knife, or just for the Consecration, for example, with pen and ink on a blade, to be washed off during the Consecration or afterwards.}

Note: Whatever you put on the tool should be well-researched and personal to you. Don't just pick some symbol as a sigil because you like it. Know what that symbol means and what Energies you are permanently putting into your tool by using that symbol. A sigil is a drawn symbol which has meaning for the person using it and possibly also for the world at large. It can be similar to a magickal trademark, or it can be used to show affinities and alliances, such as using an owl as a sigil symbolizing wisdom or the Goddess Athena. Some people use a rune or letter of some other magickal alphabet as their sigil. Some Traditions have their own sigil which is used by all members. Also, any magickal name or motto you choose should be well researched and one you can live with as the years go by. You can also Consecrate an item without using any sort of sigil, name or motto. The very act of Consecration puts your personal Energy into the item and magickally "marks" it as yours.

(Step 3) <u>Cast a Circle</u>:
{Cast in the manner you are accustomed to, or use the Generic Wiccan Circle, as described earlier.}

(Step 4) <u>The Goddess and God are Called into the Circle</u>:
{Call in the manner you are accustomed to, or again, you can use the Generic Wiccan Circle, as described above.}

(Step 5) <u>Cleanse the Tool with Earth and Water</u>:
{Once you have the Circle up and the Gods called, you take the item and psychically "cleanse" it by taking the salted water and running it over the item with your fingers, to remove unwanted or stray influences.}
Note: You can wipe the salt water off afterward if it might damage the item.

(Step 6) <u>Cleanse the Tool with Fire and Air</u>:
{Psychically Cleanse the item again with the lit incense, running it through the smoke.}
Note: *By doing these two actions, the item is Cleansed with all four elements.*

(Step 7) <u>Affirm why you are doing this Working</u>:
{Now say a short affirmation and statement of purpose, such as:}

> *"This is my sacred Athame.*
> *May it serve me well in my magickal Workings,*
> *and may the Goddess and God aid me in my Workings."*

(Step 8) <u>Anoint your Tool</u>:
{Now take the oil and anoint the item while putting your Energy into it, concentrating on the uses you will have for

the tool and how it will aid you and be attuned to your personal Energies.}

Note: You can wipe the oil off afterward. You don't need large amounts of salt water or oil, just enough to place some of each on the item and let the Energies of the liquids be "absorbed" into the item.

(Step 9) <u>Seal your Work</u>:
{Once all the Cleansing has been done, you should lay the tool on your Pentacle so it can be Grounded, or "Sealed" for your purposes.}

Note: You can consecrate more than one tool at a time, one after the other, but it is not recommended to do too many at any one time, because you can get "burned out," and the last consecrations might not be as effective as the earlier ones in the same Working. In our classes we have students Consecrate their four main tools in one Working, and perhaps one or two more, but no more than that.

(Step 10) <u>Finish the Ritual and Open the Circle</u>:
{Once you are finished with the Consecration you then Ground any excess Energy through the Pentacle and close down the circle as usual. You are Done.}

Once your Tools are Consecrated, they should be stored where they will be protected and out of the way, so they will not be handled by just anyone. Most people have some sort of sheath for their Athame (which also makes it easier to wear and carry), and at the minimum wrap their other tools in silk. If you have a permanent Altar, placing your tools there is a good thing. Some people have a ritual bag or small suitcase in which they store their Tools and garb and the other items they bring to rituals. A special storage drawer or box might be better for you. Whatever suits you and your living space is fine, just so the Tools are safely stored and out of the way.

PROBLEM SOLVING USING MAGICK

Defining the problem is the first step in doing any spell or Working. Once you have precisely defined a problem, you are usually halfway toward solving it. Focusing the mind and will are necessary for the successful practice of magick. This is one way of doing it.

Wiccans are very careful when performing magick. They strive to effect an outcome, yet not dictate exactly how it is to be done. This attitude leaves openings for possibilities which the magician might not have considered, but which might be better for all concerned. Sometimes a Wiccan has to do less of a spell than they might wish.

There was a Wiccan whose daughter was dating an extremely unsavory character, a criminal very unpleasant to be around. He would sponge off of the daughter, taking advantage of her good nature, and visit the Wiccan's house at all hours. The Wiccan wanted the daughter to stop seeing this man. But to do a Working to that effect would have been Black Magick, forcing the daughter to stop seeing this man against her will, or forcing the man to stop seeing the daughter. We were called in to help. Sometimes it helps to have an outside party to give perspective. After talking to the Wiccan the following was determined: The Wiccan didn't want this person around and wished the daughter would see for herself just what kind of a man he was.

To address these issues we performed a twofold Working. The first part was shielding the Wiccan's home and property against the boyfriend. So the boyfriend would feel extremely unpleasant if he came on the property or into the house, we created a Shield like a psychic "unwelcome" mat. This is perfectly acceptable, as people certainly have the right to protect their property and decide which people to allow in their home. This Shield was especially extended to the telephone line, so the boyfriend would be reluctant to call.

The second part of the Working was done to send Energy to the cosmos to allow the daughter to see this man as he was, get a good look at his real character. If the daughter was, even unconsciously, discontented with her relationship, this could give her the energy to see him as he truly was and start to break his hold over her.

The first part of the spell worked very well. The daughter had been sneaking the boyfriend into the house while the Wiccan was away, or at night when everyone else was sleeping. He also called at all hours. These activities stopped almost immediately. He just didn't feel like coming around or calling anymore.

The second part took longer. After about six months, the daughter announced she was not seeing the boyfriend anymore, and had not for several months. When questioned why, she said she had observed him cheat a friend out of some money, and had seen other ways in which the boyfriend was dishonest and cruel to others. Eventually she realized he was pulling these things on her also. She was about to drop him when he up and left her, because he just didn't want to see her anymore.

Now, whether all this was the direct result of the spells cannot be said for sure. But the daughter did stop seeing this boyfriend, and he did stop coming to the house and phoning.

THE BELIEF FACTOR

Magick works only when the practitioner believes in it. You have to believe what you are doing. If you scoff or doubt, the Energy will not do what you want. Your concentration will be divided between the spell and your doubts. Coincidences may happen, but to some Wiccans, there are no coincidences. Everything happens for a purpose. Sometimes you never find out what the purpose is, and sometimes you do. *"Sometimes the magick works, and sometimes it doesn't."* There are always larger forces working of which you might not be aware.

In the end, the way to judge the effectiveness of magick is, did the job get done? Whether the agent of accomplishment is yourself, the person you did the Working for, or a totally random factor, if the job gets done, the magick was successful.

Another factor is expressed in the saying, *"The Gods help those who help themselves."* You can do all the job-finding spells in the world, but to be effective you also have to pick up the paper, make some calls, get dressed up, go to the interviews, and present yourself in a favorable light. The Gods will not rain dollar bills on you from the blue. But if you do the magick and then go out and apply yourself, you can increase your effectiveness much more than if you did not do the magick. Maybe it is because the magick helps concentrate your intent and goals. Maybe it is because the magick works to make you irresistible to prospective employers. Maybe the magick helps put you in the right place at the right time and allows you to maximize your chances. In the end, it really doesn't matter as long as you got the job you wanted.

WORKING A SPELL

There are four elements to Working a spell: to Will, to Know, to Do, and to Keep Silent.

1. **"To Will"** comes from having a firm resolve and a clear idea of what is to be accomplished, and the belief that what you are doing will work.

2. **"To Know"** has a twofold meaning: to know what is to be accomplished, to have a clear idea of just what is needed, and, to know how to do the spell itself.

3. **"To Do"** is just that, doing the spell. Spells are not mere wishes. You have to put Energy into the system to effect change. How much you *do* may have a direct correlation to how quickly and thoroughly you get results.

4. **"To Keep Silent"** means not to talk or brag about what you did. Just quietly go about your normal business and be pleasantly surprised when you discover that what you Willed has come to pass, though not always in the form you imagined. Keeping silent can be the most important, for once you do the spell and release the Energy, your constant talking about and dwelling upon the subject can cause the spell to fizzle or backfire. If you are thinking about it, your thoughts haven't let go, so the spell has never been properly sent on its way. If you talk about it, you might let it slip to the wrong ears, and Energy might be put into fighting the spell, whether the person who heard is affected or just a concerned well-wisher. Usually, after a magickal Working, most Wiccans will engage in the most mundane of tasks, like cleaning or other routine chores which occupy the mind and get their thoughts off the magick just performed. This creates a mental break between the practitioner and the Energy sent, so the thoughts of the sender pulling on and inhibiting the

actions desired. It also can make for a cleaner house and more orderly living environment! Being active is an important key here. Just sitting and watching TV will not do it, for you are not mentally and physically engaged.

Common Workings

Cleansings, Blessings, and Healings are by far the most common magickal Workings, or Spells, performed by most Wiccans. This chapter also reviews Prayer, Divination, and other forms of magick for specific purposes.

CLEANSINGS

Cleansings are used when a place, person, or item has negative or unwanted stray Energies and a "clean slate" is needed. Cleansings are usually done with the four elements, using Water, and salt (for Earth), and incense (for Air and Fire). After a circle is put up, the thing to be cleansed is first aspurged with the water and salt, and then purified with the incense smoke. As this is going on, the person performing the Cleansing should visualize the negative Energies being washed away. This should continue until it feels "clean." Sometimes, more than one Cleansing is necessary. A Cleansing is not a substitute for an exorcism, if a person or place is inhabited by unwanted entities. Exorcisms are advanced and occasionally dangerous activities, best left to those who are experienced in such matters.

Sage is an herb which is commonly used for cleansing. Smudging with sage is highly effective at chasing away unwanted Energies, smells, spirits, and other entities.

BLESSINGS

A Blessing is usually done after a Cleansing, especially on a new home or living space. After the space is cleansed, take wine and cakes, and perform the Great Rite and Blessing allowing the presence of the Goddess and God to fill the area. Ask for their protection of the space and their blessings upon all who enter and all who live there. Consecrating tokens that represent the Goddess and God is one way of maintaining their presence. These can be actual statues, pictures, or just a crystal, rock, or other item that symbolizes the Deities for you. Once the place is Cleansed and Blessed and the Circle is down, these items should be placed in a safe place, to aid in protecting and blessing the space. The Cleansing and Blessing can be renewed whenever it seems appropriate. Most do it at least once a year.

HEALINGS

Healings are a special form of Blessing and Cleansing. The recipient of the Energy should *always* be aware and willing for the Healing to be done. If the person is not present, or has not actively allowed a healing to take place, the Energy can be "sent to the Cosmos," for the person to use as s/he will (not using the Energy always being an option). Additionally, an active Healing should *never* be done on a person with a cardiovascular condition. The change in Energies could trigger a heart attack, stroke, ruptured aneurysm, or similar problem. Usually the best way is to send the Energies to the Cosmos, allowing the person to tap into the Energies as they need. This tapping into the Energies can be done consciously or unconsciously.

PRAYER AND OTHER MAGICKS

Prayer is a type of spell, because it is sending focused Energy for a specific purpose. Prayer is certainly encouraged, but be careful you are not trying to shape events to your personal purposes without the willing consent of the recipient. In this way, some types of prayers can be viewed as a form of Black Magick. If you pray for the "salvation of others" without their consent, you are trying to force your will on them. The best method is to pray to the Gods or the Cosmos for things to turn out as they should, or to go well, and let the individuals make their own choices of how that will be for them. Just "sending Energy" for the use of whomever is another generic type of prayer which does not involve unwanted coercion. Otherwise, just asking, "May I pray for you?" is acceptable.

"Magick is the controlled use of will to effect change in a person or the world." It can be a powerful tool and should be used with caution and respect for what it can accomplish. As the saying goes, *"Be careful what you wish for, for you just might get it."* And just because you have an immediate need or want, the future may bring different circumstances that change your wishes and needs considerably. The best thing is to work for change within yourself, working toward self-betterment and refinement of the soul. Remember the political slogan "Think Globally, Act Locally"? If you effect change within yourself, you change a little bit of your local part of the world. And when you change the world locally, you change the world!

DIVINATION

Another form of magick and spell work which Wiccans use is "Divination." Divination helps find answers, predict the future, find out what other people are thinking or doing, and get advice about things. Wiccans are not specifically required to do divination, but most do. You do not have to put up a circle for divination, but if you do, you will find that outside distractions are greatly minimized, you can concentrate better, and you will probably get better results. Divinatory systems are not worshipped in themselves, but are tools for self-improvement, and gaining insight into one's self, motivations, and possible strengths and weaknesses.

Wiccans use most every divinatory method which is known to the modern world. Most will preferably use a tool (like tarot cards or astrological charts) or device (like a magickal mirror or pendulum) to focus upon for divination.

The most common divinatory system used by Wiccans is tarot, which is a set of cards with symbols and pictures. When properly used, it can help the unconscious mind work out problems, help others, and discover information about the past, present, and future. Some Wiccans make money "telling fortunes" with the tarot. Most, however, use the tarot only as a self-guidance tool and will not take money if they do readings for others. Other divinatory systems used by Wiccans include astrology, the Norse runes, and scrying, which uses something like a crystal ball to focus upon for symbol-impressions.

There are "natural psychics" in Wicca, but they are few and far between. If you use something outside yourself, it becomes easier to control the experience. One note: Most Wiccans do not use or recommend using *Ouija*™ boards, or practicing the Spiritualist's techniques known as "Table Tapping" or "Spirit Spelling." These can be effective, and they require little or no skill, but unless used in a controlled environment (like a protected circle), they can allow discarnate entities to come through and possibly cause trouble, including even "possession," on rare occasions. For these and other reasons, we consider these practices potentially dangerous.

What form of divination a Wiccan might practice is entirely up to the individual. Many different methods are available, and it is best to experiment with a practice to test its effectiveness. There are many books available which detail the "how to" of all sorts of methods. Try to avoid spending lots of money on something, however, until you are sure you'll like it. Using a pendulum is one method which requires little cost or training. Paul always carries a pendant on a cord with him, which he uses as a pendulum for divination. He holds the cord and asks, "What is your yes? What is your no?" and observes how the pendulum moves in response for each question. Then come the questions.

It is perfectly acceptable to test a divinatory system, especially the pendulum. Asking two mutually exclusive questions like "Will I go to New York next week?" and then, "Will I stay in town all next week?" can help test if you are getting a true reading. Writing down the questions before-hand can help organize your thoughts. And writing down the answers and keeping track of their accuracy can also show if this is the system for you. This then becomes a part of your Book of Shadows.

Both Paul and Estelle practice several different forms of divination depending on the type of information desired and the time and materials available. But divination can become a crutch, and you should save it for the big stuff, or when you are truly stuck with a choice and cannot get a good take on which option might be better. If you end up doing a divination every morning before you get dressed or go out, you are doing it too much. If you cannot simply get through life without divination to help you make decisions, then it is becoming more of a handicap than help, and you should stop. But divination is a very ancient tool, and if used carefully, it can be an effective aid in helping you make some of your life choices.

How divination works is debated. Some say when you use any form of divination you are really just tapping into your own subconscious intuition and actually guiding yourself. Some feel they are receiving advise directly from the Gods, or a guardian angel, or even perhaps dead Aunt Minnie. The Gods are good guides and a guardian angel might be helpful. However, it is best to leave dead Aunt Minnie out of it. She probably has other things to do.

Occasionally, it can help to get perspective by having someone else read for you, but it is not wise to make it a habit. If you do it for yourself, you are learning a skill and getting more in touch with your inner self, which aids in the self-betterment Great Work process. It is better if you put in the Energy yourself, because it will probably be a better reading. Remember, "The Gods help those who help themselves."

Conclusion

In these pages we have attempted to outline the religion and lifestyle of Wicca as it is practiced now around the Millennium. Wicca is a changing and growing lifestyle loosely allied to the New Age and Earth Spirituality movements that can be described as a disciplined Spiritual Path for those who want to take charge and be personally responsible for their own beliefs. Wicca is not a path for everyone. But those who choose this path must decide for themselves what to believe and how to practice those beliefs. Those who consciously choose to will discover how empowering this decision can be.

Wicca also entails a great deal of personal responsibility, for each Wiccan must ultimately take credit or blame for all they do, or do not do, in their life. Taking responsibility mandates that one live one's life fully, remaining conscious and aware of all which transpires. Habit, routine, and ruts all dull awareness and lull a person into somnambulence. These are the enemies of conscious living and of all Wiccans.

Wicca is a tolerant path which respects all spiritual beliefs. It honors both diversity and commonality—of beliefs, of practices, of ways of living on this Earth—which we share not only with our fellow Wiccans, but with the followers of all other Earth-centered religions.

People who practice Wicca tend to be individualists and independent. This we celebrate. Wiccans definitely don't follow the crowd, nor make their life decisions based upon the fads of the mundane world. Yet we Wiccans have our own fads and trends and societal norms. They're just somewhat different from those of the mainstream.

As we have tried to illustrate in this book, Wicca is in many ways a Path of dichotomies and contradictions. But now, at the turn of the Millennium, we are all experiencing many contradictions in our daily lives.

What the next hundred years will bring to Wicca is as yet unknown, but that we will survive another hundred years is certain. Witchcraft has proved endlessly adaptable as a religion and this is its main strength. But this adaptability has been called wishy-washiness. Wiccans are accused of an absence of absolutes or morals. Admittedly, the fact that Wicca is so diverse and non-centralized is both an asset and liability. But as people grow and progress, those who choose their own spiritual path find it a disciplined process for seeking and choosing, trying and testing, accepting and rejecting, finding and claiming beliefs and practices appropriate for themselves. Their faith will be all the stronger for the empowered way they have chosen to live their lives. In the end, Wicca is just a Path of choice, conscious and deliberate. And the rewards of Wicca are awareness and empowerment.

May the Goddess and God watch over you and guide you in your seeking.

BLESSED BE.

Bibliography

Adler, Margot. *Drawing Down The Moon*. Beacon Press: Boston, 1979.

Apuleius, Lucius: Robert Graves (tr.) *The Golden Ass*. Penguin Books: Middlesex, UK. 1950.

Bidart, Gay-Darlene. *The Naked Witch*. Pinnacle Books: New York, 1975.

Buckland, Raymond. *The Tree: The Complete Book of Saxon Witchcraft*. Samuel Weiser Inc.: New York, 1974.

Gardner, Gerald R. *High Magic's Aid*. Houghton Mifflin Co.: London, 1949.

Gardner, Gerald R. *Witchcraft Today*. Rider: London, 1954.

Leek, Sybil. *The Complete Art of Witchcraft: Penetrating the Secrets of White Witchcraft*. Harper & Row: New York, 1971.

Leyland, Charles G. *Aradia: or the Gospel of the Witches*. (originally published in 1890) Phoenix Publishing: Custer, WA, 1990.

Starhawk. *The Spiral Dance: A Rebirth of the Ancient Religion of The Great Goddess*. Harper Collins Publishers: New York, 1979.

Index